THE SECRET SYLLABUS

SKILLS FOR SCHOLARS

The Secret Syllabus: A Guide to the Unwritten Rules of College Success, Jay Phelan and Terry Burnham

The Economist's Craft: An Introduction to Research, Publishing, and Professional Development, Michael S. Weisbach

The Book Proposal Book: A Guide for Scholarly Authors, Laura Portwood-Stacer

The Princeton Guide to Historical Research, Zachary M. Schrag

You Are What You Read: A Practical Guide to Reading Well, Robert DiYanni

Super Courses: The Future of Teaching and Learning, Ken Bain

Syllabus: The Remarkable, Unremarkable Document That Changes Everything, William Germano and Kit Nicholls

Leaving Academia: A Practical Guide, Christopher L. Caterine

A Field Guide to Grad School: Uncovering the Hidden Curriculum, Jessica McCrory Calarco

How to Think like Shakespeare: Lessons from a Renaissance Education, Scott Newstok

The Craft of College Teaching: A Practical Guide, Robert DiYanni and Anton Borst

Will This Be on the Test? What Your Professors Really Want You to Know about Succeeding in College, Dana T. Johnson with Jennifer E. Price

Praise for

THE SECRET SYLLABUS

"*The Secret Syllabus* is unlike any other book I've read on preparing for college success. The stories and conversations are enjoyable and the authors don't just give advice, they explain how to do it. If you have questions about the culture of your college before you even get started, this book is a must-read."

—**Shellee Howard**, CEO of College Ready

"Uniquely personal and exquisitely readable. Navigating the 'secret curriculum' of higher education is nebulous and difficult, but aspiring college students should look no further than *The Secret Syllabus* to set themselves up for a successful (and happy) journey forward. This is a book I wish I had when I was starting out in college."

—**Sagar Desai**, MD, Teach For America

"*The Secret Syllabus* should have been titled *Rules for Life*. The authors take us on a tour of student life in academia and distill the skills necessary for freshmen to thrive. At a time when students seem increasingly ridden with anxiety, this book throws them a lifeline they can grasp. I will definitely recommend this book to my freshmen."

—**Daniele Struppa**, President of Chapman University

"I speak with many college students who are interested in the FBI's Behavioral Analysis Unit. I will add this book to the list of must-reads. Phelan and Burnham have written a dynamic road map for successfully navigating the challenging college years. From setting goals to career planning and every step in between, they are there guiding you with specific, actionable behaviors you *should* do to achieve your goals and dreams."

—**Kristen Slater**, Special Agent and Unit Chief of the FBI's Behavioral Analysis Unit

"*The Secret Syllabus* covers it all, from the big ideas for living life fully to the small navigations of daily college life. It's a great read for students looking for the 'secrets' for success in college and choosing a career path that is the right fit for them. Who wouldn't want that?"

—**Roxanne G. Neal**, Assistant Dean and Director of the New Student and Transition Programs at UCLA

"I know from my twenty years of experience teaching at Harvard that academic excellence requires far more than acing the material. *The Secret Syllabus* will teach you how to create positive and effective relationships with your faculty. You will learn how to talk to your professors, what to do in office hours, how to stay in touch without being a burden, and much, much more."

—**Carole Hooven**, Codirector of Undergraduate Studies, Department of Human Evolutionary Biology, Harvard University

THE SECRET SYLLABUS

A Guide to the
Unwritten Rules of
College Success

Jay Phelan &
Terry Burnham

PRINCETON UNIVERSITY PRESS

Princeton and Oxford

Published by Princeton University Press
41 William Street, Princeton, New Jersey 08540
99 Banbury Road, Oxford OX2 6JX

press.princeton.edu

All Rights Reserved

Library of Congress Cataloging-in-Publication Data

Names: Phelan, Jay, author. | Burnham, Terry, author.
Title: The secret syllabus : a guide to the unwritten rules of
    college success / Jay Phelan and Terry Burnham.
Description: Princeton, New Jersey : Princeton University Press, 2022. |
    Series: Skills for scholars | Includes bibliographical references and index.
Identifiers: LCCN 2021049279 (print) | LCCN 2021049280 (ebook) |
    ISBN 9780691224428 (paperback) | ISBN 9780691224404 (hardcover) |
    ISBN 9780691224411 (ebook)
Subjects: LCSH: College student orientation—United States. |
    Academic achievement—United States. | Study skills—United States. |
    BISAC: EDUCATION / Higher | STUDY AIDS / College Guides
Classification: LCC LB2343.32 .P54 2022 (print) | LCC LB2343.32 (ebook) |
    DDC 378.1/980973—dc23/eng/20211116
LC record available at https://lccn.loc.gov/2021049279
LC ebook record available at https://lccn.loc.gov/2021049280

British Library Cataloging-in-Publication Data is available

Editorial: Peter Dougherty, Alena Chekanov
Production Editorial: Terri O'Prey
Text and Cover Design: Chris Ferrante
Production: Erin Suydam
Publicity: Alyssa Sanford, Kathryn Stevens
Copyeditor: Michelle Garceau Hawkins

Jacket image: Shutterstock

This book has been composed in Source Serif 4, Source Sans, and Alternate Gothic

Printed on acid-free paper. ∞

Printed in the United States of America

10 9 8 7 6 5 4 3 2 1

Contents

The Nuts and Bolts of Learning and Performing

Overcoming Barriers to Success

Career Planning

Conclusion

Preface

Speaking to the Women's Club of Rio de Janeiro in 1954, the anthropologist Kalervo Oberg presented the idea of "culture shock" for the very first time.

Culture shock is precipitated by the anxiety that results from losing all our familiar signs and symbols of social intercourse. These signs or cues include the thousand and one ways in which we orient ourselves to the situations of daily life . . . All of us depend for our peace of mind and our efficiency on hundreds of these cues, most of which we do not carry on the level of conscious awareness.

Now when an individual enters a strange culture, all or most of these familiar cues are removed. He or she is like a fish out of water. No matter how broad-minded or full of good will you may be, a series of props have been knocked from under you, followed by a feeling of frustration and anxiety.

Oberg was addressing the wives of American engineers who had recently been stationed in Brazil. His intention was to help them better understand what they were experiencing as they struggled to adapt to life in another culture, far from what they had considered "home."

The anthropologist just as easily could have been describing the "Welcome to College" situation that occurs each fall on campuses across the world. Because college, too, is a foreign culture to the newly arriving students and, as with other cultures, it operates with written, as well as unwritten, rules.

Not knowing these rules and norms can lead to frustration and disappointment. Conversely, learning these rules—especially those of the unwritten variety—has important practical implications for students, enhancing their ability to thrive and to enjoy improved opportunities and outcomes.

———————

Our book, *The Secret Syllabus: A Guide to the Unwritten Rules of College Success*, had its origins in a situation that was superficially very different from that of the engineers' wives. Yet it was, in fact, uncannily similar. We—your authors, Jay and Terry—having already struggled through our own college experiences (described in the introduction), found ourselves immersed in new and different roles in the world of higher education.

While we were graduate students, our roles required us to mentor and help undergraduates as we lived alongside them in one of Harvard's diverse, vibrant, and close-knit residential communities. As resident advisors, our responsibilities included teaching undergraduate courses and nurturing students' academic lives. But our purview extended far beyond the intellectual, encompassing their social and cultural development, and even their recreation and physical well-being.

It was almost as if we had been given the chance for a "do-over" of college—but with an important mission for the second go-round. We had the responsibility of helping students benefit from the lessons that we had (eventually) learned, after stumbling through things the first time.

Embedded within the undergraduates' world, we experienced a dawning awareness that our students were all deep in an unfamiliar new culture. Infinite varieties of our own past difficulties were playing out in their lives. And that realization made clear that the long catalog of missteps, wrong turns, wasted opportunities, and regrettable decisions that we each carried reflected our own time as strangers in a strange land.

This book, *The Secret Syllabus: A Guide to the Unwritten Rules of College Success*, represents our distilled wisdom about how to improve student success. Our goal is to help students learn and adapt to their new culture faster, flourishing with less stress and struggle than they would otherwise experience.

College is a challenging and sometimes opaque culture; there's no getting around this. But with thoughtful, engaged, considerate, and persistent commitment to understanding the culture, your rewards and satisfaction will be considerable.

———————

College is many things, and it is not monolithic. There are commuter colleges and liberal arts schools. There are research-based institutions and community colleges. There are urban and rural colleges. All colleges, however, are fundamentally different from high school.

Arriving at college, students enter a culture defined not simply by academic substance, but also by a different set of social rules and norms, whose navigation requires craft and whose successful mastery empowers students in becoming full partners in their educations.

We hope that you will think of this book as a conversation with two guides who have mastered the ways of this alien culture. OK, perhaps not "mastered," but we have at least made some progress in that general direction. We're inviting you to join our conversation as the beginning of a larger conversation in which you, the student, become an engaged and enthusiastic participant.

We have a unique perspective on college culture. We have been actively engaged in learning and teaching cultural navigation for more than three decades, beginning together as graduate students and progressing through the faculty ranks. Importantly—and in contrast to most professors and counselors—we have spent more than a little time at the wrong end of the curve, and we have faced the highs and lows of success and failure in academics and life.

Our journey has taken a winding path, from the isolation and anxiety faced by many first-generation students through transcripts littered with F's and academic probation (*really*) to receiving our PhDs from Harvard.

We know what it feels like to sit in the back row of classes that don't seem relevant to us and to listen to instructors out of touch with our own experiences in the world. But we also understand how to regroup and reflect, how to think critically, how to learn, and how to overcome the greatest challenges, and to excel as fully engaged participants in our education when it matters.

Because the book is so personal, we include firsthand stories throughout. This will require you to shift perspectives occasionally, as the conversation moves between Jay's and Terry's first-person accounts and other stories about our students and colleagues.

———

There is no shortage of college advice literature. Books, websites, academic advising publications, and blogs abound. Expert columns from magazines and professional periodicals, too, promise guidance. But we are not simply compiling a collection of tips and tricks, or hacks that, once memorized, will ensure your success. *The Secret Syllabus* is a different type of book.

We are introducing you to a complex culture and your role within it. This is done best through a conversation, itself a central feature of college culture: stories, wrapped in discussion and analysis of ideas, conveying fundamental foundational principles. This approach generates a framework for addressing—and answering—the questions of how to succeed within the culture.

This approach also distinguishes *The Secret Syllabus* from such laundry lists of disconnected bits of advice. While they can be helpful, such tips and tricks are limited descriptors of the culture of college. Necessarily incomplete and inefficient, they inevitably prove inadequate. Instead, we'll teach you to develop your own rules of behavior based on a deeper understanding of the culture.

Here's an example. Suppose you're preparing for an exam. If a tutor merely provides the answers to a list of study questions, that will help you only if those exact questions appear on the test. (They won't.) If the tutor instead teaches you the concepts addressed in the course, and how to apply that knowledge to solve the study questions, it doesn't matter whether those questions appear on the test. You're prepared for any question.

Our approach is designed for all students. There is an important and growing recognition that within educational settings there are assumptions, expectations, academic norms, and social rules that are not explicitly conveyed. This secret information—a "hidden curriculum"—can reinforce social inequalities and disproportionately harm students, particularly those from disadvantaged backgrounds and first-generation students.

But even well-prepared students from outstanding high schools can, and often do, have trouble adapting to college, for many reasons, including that the pace of instruction, directed by academic researchers, is both faster and more demanding for long-term thinking.

While our perspective of "college as an alien culture" will have significant value for students from groups underrepresented in higher education, including first-generation students, it is not limited to them. In exploring and revealing the culture of college, we seek to illuminate not just its secret information, but all dimensions of the largely unwritten rules and norms governing the culture.

When first describing the phenomenon of culture shock, the anthropologist Oberg took care to note that "Only with a complete grasp of all the cues of social intercourse will this strain disappear." We hope that with this book you find all that you need to achieve this.

But we also aspire for more. We hope that you come to recognize that the strategies that you will learn—and the deep understanding that will equip you to develop additional strategies on your own—can, with very little modification, help you succeed in the world beyond college.

THE SECRET SYLLABUS

THE BIG PICTURE

Every Culture Has Rules and Norms. Some Are Written, But Many Are Not

One fall day, some years ago, Terry was sitting in his office at Harvard University near the Charles River. Within one minute (literally), he received two nearly identical requests:

> *Dear Professor Burnham, I am applying to graduate school and I would appreciate if you would write a recommendation letter on my behalf. Sincerely, your former student.*

To one of the students, Terry wrote, "Yes. It would be my pleasure to write a letter for you. Please come by my office sometime this week. We can discuss my letter and I'll help you develop a strategy to get accepted." To the other student he wrote, "I'm sorry. Unfortunately, I won't be able to help you at this time."

Both students had taken the same class with Terry. And the student who received the "Not at this time" response had even earned a higher grade than the student who received the "I will help you."

What was going on? How is it possible that a student who performed less well can get valuable career assistance and a recommendation letter, while a better-performing student does not? This seeming paradox is resolved by understanding and following some unstated cultural norms regulating behavior in college.

Grades are important, but they are not everything. Far from it, in fact. The best outcomes require artful navigation of the unique college culture. *The Secret Syllabus* is a guide to mastering these unstated cultural norms that lead to academic (and life) success. With it, you won't lose your way.

Together, we have taught more than 20,000 students at Harvard, UCLA, Pepperdine, the University of Michigan, Chapman University, and MIT. Almost every day, we encounter students who work harder and achieve less than they would if they knew and understood the material in *The Secret Syllabus*.

Additionally, during college, we—the authors, Jay Phelan and Terry Burnham—made some avoidable and spectacularly terrible choices. These blunders caused us to miss opportunities and to waste untold time—sometimes hours, sometimes months—in aimless and unproductive floundering. We needed this book!

Before laying out the book's structure, let's start with a bit of biography.

Jay grew up in California and attended UCLA. He then earned a master's degree at Yale, followed by his doctorate in biology at Harvard. Jay taught at Harvard and Pepperdine before returning to teach biology at UCLA and write biology textbooks.

Terry grew up near Detroit and attended the University of Michigan. He earned a master's degree at San Diego State University and a second master's at MIT, followed by his doctorate in business economics at Harvard. Terry was a professor at the Harvard Business School, the Harvard Kennedy School, and the University of Michigan, before moving to California to teach finance at Chapman University.

You can be forgiven for assuming that two Harvard PhDs must have skated through school and so cannot understand the issues of typical students. This could not be further from the truth. We have certainly had some great outcomes, but, for the most part, we have been depressingly average in the mistakes that we've made.

Let's start with Jay in his own words:

I was not a good student. Almost from the day I arrived at college (as a first-generation college student), things went poorly for me. My courses didn't speak to me. It felt as though my instructors weren't telling me anything about my life. My textbooks seemed out of touch with my own personal experiences in the world. And consequently, little of my course work felt relevant to me. I wanted to check out. Not surprisingly, my resulting "strategy" of poor attendance led to some very bad outcomes.

This wasn't simply a brief, difficult transition to college. I spent years stumbling into and out of "academic probation" and the more dire "subject to dismissal." I was an interdisciplinary disappointment and received the dreaded grade of F repeatedly.

I understand what it is like to sit in class and feel that all hope is lost. But I also have learned how to turn things around.

And from Terry:

I never saw a clear and obvious path when I set off for college. Initially, I was pre-med because my father wanted me to be a doctor. After getting accepted to medical school, however, I decided to instead try to find my own path.

I was a computer programmer, a tank driver in the U.S. Marine Corps Reserves, and worked on Wall Street for Goldman, Sachs &

Co., before earning an MBA, a PhD, and then becoming a professor. My path was unnecessarily circuitous because of my lack of focus and guidance.

Uncertainty about my direction also led me to take time off from college. I lived in Salt Lake City, where I skied and worked at a variety of jobs, including as a busboy and a short-order cook. Only after taking a day labor job at a slaughterhouse and standing waist-deep among bloody carcasses did I have the epiphany that maybe college wasn't so bad.

We are not proud recounting our struggles and failures; for many years we were too embarrassed to even mention them to anyone. We only reveal them here in the hope that helping you avoid these blunders can be a silver lining.

Throughout this book, the advice and guidance we provide is not always available from your instructors. Your challenges may be motivation, time management, life pressures, study skills, mentor-seeking, finding a learning community, or something else.

You may feel like you don't know what you should be doing. Or you may know what you should be doing, but don't quite know how to do it effectively. These challenges can be exacerbated because, in many cases, your instructors have never faced similar issues.

For example, while more than a third of all college students have parents who do not have a bachelor's degree, only a tiny percentage of faculty members were first-generation students. It's hard to find your way, let alone thrive, when you're not quite sure that you belong and may lack a sufficiently knowledgeable support network.

The experiences of struggling, juggling, searching, and bouncing back from setbacks may be unfamiliar to many professors, but we know these issues intimately. We have wrestled with (and overcome) these challenges.

Advice Is Not Enough

Much of the advice that students receive about how to be more successful in college is not particularly useful:

"You should go to office hours." *This is true, but it's not very helpful. Because once you're there, what should you do? Here's a hint: asking your instructor to re-explain concepts from class is not among the most valuable reasons to go to office hours.*

"You should get some research experience." "You should get some real-world experience, like an internship." "You should get a faculty mentor." "You should be more efficient when you study." *Again, these are true. But they miss the mark. As is often the case, the more important guidance you need is about **how** you actually do those things. We will help you succeed with all of these.*

Our overriding goal in *The Secret Syllabus* is to highlight the ideas and practices that you are not likely to come up with on your own. We get particularly excited about counterintuitive solutions, those for which your instincts might lead you to do exactly the wrong thing, even after careful consideration.

"The sooner you have a major, the better a candidate you will be for jobs, for transfer to a better school, or for graduate schools." *Not only is this advice not helpful, in a very large number of cases, it is completely wrong.*

And still other advice—although undeniably reasonable—is just too obvious to be helpful. For example, here are some actual recommendations from other college guidebooks:

> *"Get to class early."*
> *"Be prepared. Read the assigned material."*
> *"Try not to cram for tests."*
> *"Avoid procrastination."*

Moreover, we will never suggest that doing well in college simply boils down to a set of tricks or "hacks." Doing well in college, as in life, does involve learning some important tactics and skills (which we will cover). But reading or memorizing a bunch of unrelated bits of advice from a list of "tips" can take you only so far. Real success requires engagement with the substance and a foundation of deeper, guiding principles.

The Secret Syllabus

With *The Secret Syllabus* our goal is considerably more ambitious than the dispensing of advice. We want to serve as guides and, hopefully, mentors, as you become immersed in a new, complex culture. Across each of the eighteen chapters—think of them as "lectures"—our objective is to illuminate the fundamental foundational principles that will enable you to succeed, as you:

- craft your college experience;
- develop professional relationships;
- achieve academic excellence;
- increase your resiliency; and
- plan your postcollege career.

Throughout this book, we'll illustrate both productive and counter-productive approaches, using true, real-life stories. And we will summarize each lesson with "Take Home Messages," distilling the ideas into clear, concise guides to action.

Our goal is to inspire you not just to get good grades, but also to learn and to grow, to recognize that you belong, and to find satisfaction and excitement in your role as a college student. Whether you are figuring out how to select a major or how to find an effective mentor, there won't be "one size fits all" solutions.

There is some creativity—even artistry—required. Our approach is to help you develop consistently winning and effective behaviors. With this wisdom, you'll be equipped to thrive in any situation.

Take Home Messages

1. In addition to the many explicit rules and requirements, college is governed by unwritten, and rarely stated, practices and cultural norms, which we reveal in this book. True and long-term success requires mastery of both types of material.

2. Almost every student arrives at college unprepared for the impending culture shock—including even those who are academically brilliant. Mastering *The Secret Syllabus* equips students for a rich college experience and a successful life.

SETTING GOALS:
IT'S NOT THE PLAN, BUT THE PLANNING

NOT HAVING A CAREER PLAN ON DAY 1 USUALLY IS BETTER THAN HAVING ONE

Would you let a ten-year-old make the most important decision of your life? Probably not. Yet many students do exactly that. Worse still, many take pride in this fact. Moreover, usually they have been encouraged to do so—even lauded—by their parents, teachers, friends, and guidance counselors.

Two students meet and start talking. The conversation turns to "What's your major?" or one of the many other variations of "What do you want to be when you grow up?"

Student One says: "I'm pre-law. I've wanted to be a federal public defender ever since I was a little girl. I've just finished a summer internship working for The Innocence Project. And for the past three years, I have volunteered at the Legal Aid Society near my parents' house. How about you?"

Student Two says, "I'm not sure what I want to do" and then feels like a loser because:

1) They don't have a plan.
2) They (feel like they) are already falling behind.

And

3) They've apparently wasted years of opportunities to get ahead.

It's only their first or second year in college, but to the second student it seems undeniable that they're already failing. They have made no progress in building their resume. Nor have they accumulated a list of achievements and experiences that demonstrate their commitment to their chosen path.

This failure, they believe, will preclude them from succeeding in the competition for graduate school admittance, a future job, and life. Or, even in their best-case scenario, this failure will make future success much more difficult and unlikely.

Student Two is mistaken.

There is a strong—and spectacularly counter-productive—cultural message about how to become successful: "Every person has a unique talent. Successful people discover their talent early in life and relentlessly pursue their passion in spite of any difficulties. Ultimately, these people win and become tremendously successful." The unstated flip side of this message is: "If you do not have a plan by age ten, you are a loser."

You have been raised against a backdrop of hundreds of stories with this same message. We'll illustrate with three: the stories of Steve Jobs, Jane Goodall, and John Harbaugh.

Steve Jobs dispensed his life advice in a famous commencement speech at Stanford University. He distilled the advice down to three stories.

Story #1. "I dropped out of Reed College . . . After six months, I couldn't see the value in it. I had no idea what I wanted to do with my life and no idea how college was going to help me figure it out. And here I was spending all of the money my [working-class] parents had saved their entire life. So, I decided to drop out."

Jobs quit but he stayed on campus. Freed from rules and restrictions, he took the classes that he liked, including calligraphy. Later Jobs had a huge impact on computer typefaces—he has been called "the Gutenberg of our times"—and also on almost everyone's appreciation for those typefaces.

Story #2. "I got fired . . . but it turned out that getting fired from Apple was the best thing that could have ever happened to me." Freed up by being fired, Jobs started an animation company and developed further skills that would contribute to his later successes when he returned to Apple.

Story #3. "About a year ago I was diagnosed with cancer. . . . You are already naked," he said. "There is no reason not to follow your heart." Jobs argued that knowing life is finite is crucial to making wise decisions.

Throughout the talk, Jobs made the point that the road he followed was difficult. "I slept on the floor in friends' rooms. I returned Coke bottles for the five cents deposits to buy food." These struggles to stay pure reinforced Jobs's message that taking the right path is hard, because others will not support you.

"Don't lose faith . . . the only way to be truly satisfied is to do what you believe is great work." Jobs summarized his advice as:

> Don't be trapped by dogma—which is living with the results of other people's thinking. Don't let the noise of others' opinions drown out your own inner voice. And most importantly, have the courage to follow your heart and intuition. They somehow already know what you truly want to become. Everything else is secondary.

Jobs ended the speech with, "Stay Hungry. Stay Foolish."

Jane Goodall is famous for her study of chimpanzees in Africa and for her advocacy for conserving the natural world. Her life story harmonizes with the message of Steve Jobs: Find your passion early in life. Struggle, ignore detractors, and succeed.

When Jane was five years old, she once disappeared for an entire day. Worried that something bad had happened, her parents searched frantically for her. It wasn't until late that night that she was found. She emerged from a chicken coop, where she had spent twelve hours observing the chickens because she was curious to learn how eggs are produced.

Jane Goodall's career and fame followed naturally from her passion to observe animals. She went to Tanzania in 1960 with little formal scientific training. Her initial plan was for a short stay, but because the chimpanzees all ran away from her, she was unable to collect any data for a full year.

But Jane Goodall did not give up. Deciding that it might help if she let the chimps habituate to her presence, she rose early every morning and spent the days out and about in the forest. (Because the forest was wet with dew in the mornings, her clothes became soaked and made her uncomfortable. She recounts that her solution was simply to take her clothes off, walk through the jungle essentially naked, and dress only after she reached her observation ridge.)

Her persistence paid off. Eventually the chimps came to accept Jane and lost their fear of her. This enabled Goodall to make the extended, meaningful observations of their social behavior that made her famous.

What is the short version of Jane Goodall's story? Identify your passion at age five. Then embrace and follow that passion relentlessly—even if that means living alone for years in African forests.

The third story is that of John Harbaugh, a famously successful football coach. John grew up in a football family; his father was a coach and his brother was a famous professional quarterback and, later, a coach.

John Harbaugh found his football passion at a very young age and began coaching at twenty-two, soon after graduating from college. His first coaching job was unpaid, and at the decidedly non-glamorous Western Michigan University.

When John told his mother that he wanted to be a coach, she conveyed her disappointment by putting her face into a plate of mashed potatoes. But Harbaugh won his mother over with his determination. "I saw that look in his eyes," she later said. "My feeling was, 'you have to do what you want to do.'"

These stories are all versions of "The American Dream." They are interesting and inspiring. And we have tremendous respect for Steve Jobs, Jane Goodall, and John Harbaugh. However, we feel that the prevalence of the myth they endorse has three costs for most people.

First, the myth establishes an unrealistic goal. Finding your dream career in elementary school is not common. It has indeed happened that someone has—in a chicken coop at age five—found a life in which they will thrive and find happiness. This is, to put it gently, very rare. Much, much more commonly, people's interests develop and change over time. They find satisfying professions only after maturing and exploring the world's rich options.

Second, the myth makes people feel bad. With so much romanticizing of the stories of people like Jane Goodall, characterized by unusually early commitment to particular careers, it's natural to feel like a failure if you've made it all the way to college but don't yet have a "plan."

Third, the myth's central tenet makes no allowance at all for the often-valuable possibility of switching career choices. Try explaining that you're contemplating changing a plan that you've previously announced.

Your grandparents, parents, and other relatives commonly will respond as if everything was already decided. You were going to become a [lawyer, doctor, businessperson]. To suggest uncertainty or a desire to change your plan—upon finding out that you don't actually enjoy chemistry, for example—can be treated like you have failed to hold up your end of an agreement.

The prospect of breaking the news to those disappointed people can be terrible, knowing that they may (perhaps only subconsciously) make you feel that you've let them down. It's doubly difficult when you may know that it's still actually possible for you to do everything necessary to complete that original plan. But don't confuse the fact that you *can* do something with a conclusion that you *should* do that thing.

Arriving at college without having picked a career is better for most students.

We make many pronouncements about what we want to do in life when we're ten or twelve or sixteen. But think about it: as a ten-year-old, how many careers do you have real awareness of? Jay knew of five. He could be an astronaut, a race car driver, a professional athlete, the president, or a doctor.

Most people, in fact, pursue jobs that the average child has never heard of, let alone considered. Should we consider these people failures because they work in professions that kids do not choose? Of course not.

A common thread of the mythical version of success is that it requires ignoring detractors. Steve Jobs tells us to quit school if you chafe at the constraints. John Harbaugh's mother face-planted in mashed potatoes upon learning of his coaching aspirations. According to the mythic path, a big hurdle on the way to happiness is parents who fail to support your inspired choices.

A more pervasive problem is that of families encouraging and supporting poor choices. No one latched onto Jay's plan when it was to be a race car driver. But from the minute he mentioned interest in maybe becoming a doctor—even though he had no real understanding about what it entailed—the amount of support, approval, and love showered on Jay from people such as his grandmother was huge.

Such adoration can be intoxicating. And it can snowball. Soon Jay's grandmother was bragging to everyone about her grandson, "the doctor"—before he had even applied for college. Later, at age seventeen, Jay joined the staff of his high school newspaper, where he immersed himself in writing. He loved it. Suggesting to his grandmother that he might want to be a journalist or some other kind of writer, however, sounded like admitting that he had failed in his "dream" of being a doctor.

Lacking external approval, Jay downplayed his writing passion and retreated back to his pre-med plan when applying to college. Everyone breathed a sigh of relief for a while, even Jay. He was "back on track."

This is not a trivial or silly issue. Students suffer under the immense and inappropriate pressure that comes from the pervasive belief that it is better to have a long-term career plan—even when just beginning college—than to not have one. And this happens at a time when they should most be encouraged in exactly the opposite direction. To say, "I'm not sure what I want to do" makes it seem as though you are in a worse position than someone who is sure what they want to do.

Worse still, the situation can be compounded by the fact that an otherwise smart and hardworking person, once committed to a plan, can find many reasons to stick with it. But they are using a poor decision-making strategy. Such a person mistakenly interprets the fact that they can articulate many reasons supporting the wisdom of their original plan as evidence that it must be the right plan.

Terry had a student, Florian, who wanted to be an orthopedic surgeon. Early in college, Florian took initiative and contacted a doctor. He was ecstatic when offered the opportunity to "shadow" the surgeon for a few days, following her through office visits and even into the operating room.

What did Florian learn? The surgeon seemed to truly love her job and she was very good at it. To Florian, however, the doctor's life seemed horrible. Day after day, she spent her hours doing mind-numbingly repetitive tasks.

Florian faced a dilemma. He had been on the "doctor path" for many years. Like Jay, Florian was already affectionately thought of as his family's doctor. He faced a critical decision. He could suppress his newly discovered aversion to the profession, or he could admit that he wanted something different.

John Maynard Keynes, the eminent economist, is widely reported to have been confronted by an antagonistic newspaper reporter. "Lord Keynes," the reporter shouted, "you change your mind all the time. Why are you so inconsistent?" Keynes reportedly replied with, "I change my mind when I have new information. What do you do, sir?"

Florian followed the metaphorical Keynesian path and ended his nascent medical career before it had officially begun. His family was sad, but they recovered and seem to still love him.

Changing career paths is psychologically costly. But not changing is costly too. About twenty percent of people experience some sort of midlife crisis. Around the age of forty-five, the end of life becomes less abstract than it was from the perspective of a twenty- or thirty-year-old.

The comical stereotype of these midlife crises is of bald, chubby men in convertible sports cars. A less humorous manifestation, however, is clinical depression. And it turns out that one of the most commonly cited explanations by people suffering from midlife depression is having chosen the wrong career.

Consider Irving's story, following his graduation from Harvard with a degree in engineering:

> After college, I was focused on making money so I got a job with a big IT consulting firm. That became my life for many years: nonstop work and my share of accolades to keep me chasing partnership. It all came crashing down after nearly working myself to death. I suffered a breakdown and was on disability for six months. I could barely eat or sleep. I thought I was dying. I needed to leave the IT field.
>
> I considered attending film school. I actually got into both UCLA and USC film schools. I also considered a career in education and got into the Harvard Graduate School of Education. But my wife was pregnant and working on her law degree, so I decided that I just had to get back on the horse.
>
> So to answer your question, I don't like my job very much. I would love to do something with a greater social impact. But in five years, I'll probably be in the same field.

It is much harder to change careers at age fifty than at age nineteen. We encourage you to take steps—akin to Florian's—to investigate several careers. It may feel like inefficient time-wasting when you could be building your resume, but life is long and your career explorations will pay off over the next few decades.

For a plan to be the *right* plan requires it to compare favorably with all of the relevant alternatives. That's why having a career plan on Day 1 is a bad idea.

Take a look at these jobs:

- software quality assurance engineer
- property manager
- database administrator
- physical therapy manager
- risk management director

They all have two things in common. First, they all were listed in *Forbes Magazine, US News and World Report,* or *CNN Money* on lists of the top ten "happiest jobs in America" and in surveys ranking career satisfaction. Second, no ten-year-old considers these options when contemplating possible careers.

You also may be unaware of many careers that would be extremely rewarding for you because they don't even exist yet! In a report from MIT, researchers found that more than sixty percent of jobs done in 2018 had not been "invented" in 1940. They also found that the rate at which existing jobs are being replaced today by completely new work is faster than ever.

"Follow your passion" can sound like courageous—even romantic—and unobjectionably wise advice. It isn't. When you are encouraged to commit to a path before you have the slightest idea of the full range of careers, you are being encouraged to limit your options. Do you honestly know what linguistics is? Or anthropology? Or cognitive science? Or classics?

So how can you step away from this (often subtle and unstated) well-intentioned, but destructive, pressure? Start by reframing the situation. Not having a plan doesn't have to mean that you aren't moving toward a goal. Redefine your conception of what constitutes valuable goals for your first years of college.

What if your goals include:

1. *exploring* the options that are open to you;
2. *learning* about career paths you have never been exposed to;
3. *investigating* fields of inquiry and subjects of academic study that are novel to you;
4. *reflecting* on why you may have "always wanted to be a . . ."

Notice that these goals differ from many goals in that they do not articulate end points, products, or achievements. They are *processes*. An important component of wise decision-making is to obtain and evaluate the appropriate information. When you do that well, the decisions you make are usually better.

In the interest of full disclosure, we must notify you of a grim reality. Without even noticing it, you may already have enjoyed years of being rewarded for articulating a plan and basking in the warmth of certainty. Jay's student, Joselyn, was eager to point out that her situation was different. "I haven't been influenced by pressure from my parents. They're refreshingly hands-off and just want me to be happy."

Since the age of twelve, however, Joselyn had professed a desire to be a psychiatrist. She had selected her major accordingly, at the time she applied to college. This, unfortunately, meant that she didn't actually have any information about whether her parents were "hands-off." They may have seemed low-pressure simply because she had done exactly what they hoped she would do—maybe even in response to subtle pressure that twelve-year-old Joselyn had not consciously detected.

"What would happen if you told your parents that you are changing your major from Psychobiology to English or History?" Jay wondered. "Then you would learn whether they truly are hands-off."

You likely will experience a disquieting—even painful—sensation as you make the brave and wise transition to a state of exploring, learning, investigating, and reflecting. But we urge you to be strong on this issue. Your future happiness depends on it. These processes are not the same as just drifting. They are active and require engagement.

You may consider saying something like the following to your parents, friends, and advisors:

- "I'm committed to finding a fulfilling career, so I want to investigate all of the options with an open mind. Be patient."
- "There are dozens of fields of study and professions that I had never even heard of before college! Doesn't it seem wise to explore a few of them, rather than excluding all of them?"
- "When am I supposed to explore my options, if not now?"
- "Mom, Dad: Did you raise me to be a thoughtful, reflective, and smart person? Then have faith that I will make you proud in how I make one of the most important decisions in my life."

What professors may be thinking (but probably won't tell you).

■ When you announce that you've wanted to be a lawyer since you were in grade school, we are not necessarily impressed by your commitment and focus. Rather, we hope you allow yourself the opportunity—now that you are an adult—to develop your interests and discover your own path. With effort and some resiliency, you can build your very own satisfying career and life.

You can learn much from others.

Here's how people describe why they love some of the jobs you haven't considered:

■ "Every day is different."–*civil engineer*
■ "I create solutions . . . and define what we're selling."–*management consultant*
■ "I'm the type of person who likes to solve puzzles in my spare time. My work is engaging. I determine how important pieces of data relate to other information, and I have to ensure flexibility and accuracy in whatever I design."–*database administrator*
■ "My job allows me to work with people and improve their lives, leaving the world a better place."–*environmental engineer*
■ "I enjoy working in different settings . . . and value having flexible hours."–*physical therapist*

One of the great resources on a college campus is the career center. Staffed by professionals who are knowledgeable about your school and extensively trained, these centers can help you with every aspect of career exploration. Whether you're looking to create your resume, learn about internships, or investigate networking opportunities, they can help you. Even if you're just curious and would like an agenda-free, exploratory discussion about how you might use their services sometime down the road, they can help you.

Take Home Messages

1. Be forewarned: there is a pervasive myth about the best version of choosing a career: "The ideal career pops into one's head sometime between age five and age ten. Obtaining success simply requires perseverance to overcome detractors until the brilliance of that juvenile decision is recognized by the world."

2. When you were young, you did not (and could not) know all your options for your major or for your career. Any decisions you made were made in the absence of sufficient knowledge about the rich and varied possibilities open to you. Only by exploring and learning about these and reflecting on what excites you and brings you fulfillment as you mature can you make good and informed decisions. College offers this opportunity. Seize it.

3. The reality of successful career choice is exactly the opposite of the myth. Finding the right career takes persistent effort and learning. Age five or ten is likely to be a poor time to pick a career. Success often requires overcoming supporters of your early and naïve decisions. There are hundreds of satisfying and rewarding careers, many of which you are unaware.

PLANNING YOUR SCHEDULE THIS TERM, THIS YEAR, AND THROUGH GRADUATION

In the later part of college, many students could improve their outcomes if they had a time machine. Almost every college movie includes a montage of cramming for a big test. Unprepared and facing big trouble, the students drink large quantities of coffee, stay up for a few days, and overcome their obstacles. Everything works out in the end.

In reality, however, many of the most important parts of college require persistent effort for years, not just "one big push" of hard work. Without a time machine, there are no remedies for some deficiencies. In this chapter, we discuss some strategies for planning ahead in your life, sketching out a game plan, and reducing your need for that time machine when graduation approaches.

"Lag time" is a formidable enemy. It is the gap between when you do something and when you experience the consequences (good or bad) of those actions. An unfortunate consequence of lag time is that it can be a brutal barrier to achieving the life you want (and maybe even deserve).

Near the end of his time at UCLA, a student named Farhan learned this lesson the hard way:

From: Farhan
Subject: Unsolicited begging for a letter of recommendation
To: Jay Phelan <jay@ucla.edu>

> Hi Dr. Phelan,
>
> It's that time of year when people you have never met shamelessly express their entitlement to you in the form of a letter of recommendation request. Imagine the gall of an effectively complete stranger demanding to add an extra obligation to your already vast plate of obligations, without offering anything tangible in return. Well, now you don't have to imagine.
>
> It's a terrible shame, really. Without the schedule conflict that precluded me from coming to office hours last quarter, there would've been a good chance that you'd be consistently delighted by my insightful questions and well-reasoned contributions to group discussions. Probably not, but at the very least, you would have remembered my name.
>
> Speaking of remembering things . . . [short paragraph recounting aspects of my class that made an impression on Farhan].
>
> I have very low expectations about this whole situation, and will not feel slighted in the least if you decide that you are unwilling or unable to write me a letter. Thanks for everything.
>
> Sincerely, Farhan D

There's no question about it, Farhan's letter is charming and well written. Nonetheless, it is Exhibit A in the case study of *"How **not** to set yourself up for success."* As he puts together his plan for persuading potential employers and grad schools of his exceptional value, some of Farhan's future will be in the hands of a person ill-equipped to sing his praises and push him to the top of the applicant ranking list.

What does lag time have to do with this? Everything. There are many things that you'll want or need someday. But, at the time you need them, you cannot simply get them. It's too late. You must have anticipated the need months or even years earlier, and have set the wheels in motion at that time.

Imagine finding yourself one day thinking:

> *"Oh no! I need a recommendation letter. Who should I ask?"*
> **Or:** *"Oh no! I need to have some research experience for my grad school application."*
> **Or:** *"Oh no! I need experiences that illustrate leadership and collaborative work skills for my business school applications."*
> **Or:** *"Oh no! I need eight more units in order to get my degree on time. And my parents already have their plane tickets for my graduation."*

If you're ever in that position, then, like Farhan, you've stacked the odds against yourself. No matter how hard you work at that last minute, or how clever you are, certain things—professional relationships, reputations, work experiences—simply take months or years to create or develop.

Your Four-Year Game Plan

You need a game plan. In fact, you need not just a single game plan, but several. Some are short-term, others much longer. In every case, you can think of it as "Present You" doing "Future You" a big favor.

We'll start by exploring the things you'll need to consider for the Four-Year Game Plan covering your time in college. We divide this into three smaller plans.

1: How will you spend your summers?
2: What nonacademic activities will you include?
3: How will you organize your curriculum across the calendar years?

Four-year planning sounds like an accountant's unintentional method for inducing sleep. The rock band Rush disagrees, singing, "If you choose not to decide, you still have made a choice . . . I will choose a path that's clear, I will choose freewill." The song's message is direct. Don't blame others for bad outcomes; make decisions and take responsibility for your life.

Here are three examples of how planning, which seems boring, can be central to success.

1. Alan Page Goes to Law School

Alan Page grew up in Ohio as a poor African American boy. He feared that he would be limited to an unpleasant future in the steel mills. "I could deal with it being dangerous. I could deal with the dirty," he said. "But I understood repetitious [labor] wasn't going to work for me."

With a combination of talent and persistent work, Page attended the University of Notre Dame, where he was an All-American on the football team. From Notre Dame, Page was drafted by the Minnesota Vikings of the National Football League. In a remarkable fourteen-year career, he was named to nine straight Pro Bowls, including one year in which he was selected as the NFL's Most Valuable Player. Page was ultimately elected to the NFL Hall of Fame.

Mindful that no one plays forever, however, "Present" Alan Page never neglected "Future" Alan Page. While he was still a professional football player, Page enrolled in, and graduated from, law school, attending classes at night and during the off-season!

Upon retirement from football, Alan Page transitioned smoothly into a storied legal career, eventually becoming the first African American to serve on the Minnesota Supreme Court. In 2018, in recognition of his twenty-two years on the state's Supreme

Court, Justice Page was awarded the Presidential Medal of Freedom, the nation's highest civilian honor.

2. Derek "Panther" Thinks about the End of College before the Start

Less famous, but equally focused on the future, is Derek, who came to Chapman University to play football and prepare for a career in finance. Chatting with his teammates, he learned about a class taught by Terry called, informally, "A Walk Down Wall Street."

This course culminates with a trip to New York and meetings with numerous investment firms. Over the years, many Chapman students have been able to launch careers with the help of finance professionals they met during the Walk Down Wall Street class.

Soon after arriving at Chapman, Derek made an appointment with Terry. Derek arrived early, introduced himself, described his career aspirations, and said, "I have heard great things about Walk Down Wall Street." Then he said, "I am a freshman. What advice do you have for me?"

Two years later, Derek returned to the same seat in Terry's office. He said, "I spoke with you two years ago and you gave me some advice. I followed all of your advice: I took the six courses you recommended, and spent a summer in one of the internships that you suggested I investigate. Now I would like to: a) thank you, and b) apply for the Walk Down Wall Street course."

Terry literally said, "Where is the camera? No student in the history of the world has ever come to my office, asked for advice, followed that advice, and then returned. This must be a prank."

But Derek was indeed for real. So, Terry accepted him into the course and helped him to get the most out of the experience.

Today, Derek is enjoying exactly the sort of finance career he hoped for when he arrived on campus.

Do you find this story inspiring or terrifying? Perhaps terrifying, as it is unlikely that you will know what you want to do when you are first at college. (In fact, as we argue in the previous chapter, having a plan too early in life is generally a bad idea.)

The specifics of Derek's case, however, are not what is important here. Rather, the inspirational core of his story is about the huge value of even a tiny amount of planning ahead. Thirty minutes of Derek's time put him in the top one percent of all college students for increasing the likelihood of getting the outcome he wanted.

3. Alex Honnold Becomes an "Instant" Success, after 17 Years

Story number three demonstrates that planning can even lead to fame and staying alive. Alex Honnold completed the first—and only—free solo ascent of El Capitan, a 3,000-foot-high vertical rock formation in Yosemite. In free solo, a climber climbs without any ropes or tools. Just hands, mind, and a bag of chalk. One mistake can equal death.

Ominously, Honnold has said, "Every person I know who has made free soloing a big part of their life is dead."

In 2011, *Alpinist Magazine* noted that Honnold had become an "instant" success in the mountain climbing world. "In 2006, nobody had heard of him. In 2007, he free soloed Yosemite's Astroman and the Rostrum in a day, matching Peter Croft's legendary 1987 feat."

But that's not quite right. It did *appear* that Honnold had become an instant success in 2007. The reality, however, is exactly the opposite. Honnold first climbed in 1990, at the age of five, when his mother took him to a rock-climbing gym. By the age ten, he was spending several days a week climbing at a gym. So Honnold's "instant" success of 2007 actually came after 17 years of persistent work.

Alex Honnold succeeded because he planned ahead. The time frame of his planning ranged from seconds (Where is my next hand hold?) to years (What steps do I have to take to be able to free solo El Capitan?). And now to decades: Alex has developed his passion for environmental preservation and helping those less fortunate by creating the Honnold Foundation, which funds projects that bring solar power to underprivileged areas.

Alan Page went to law school while playing professional football. In his first days at college, Derek thought ahead to life after college. Alex Honnold is alive today because he looks ahead in a systematic and persistent manner.

How Will You Spend Your Summers?

One element of your Four-Year Game Plan is this: How will you utilize summers? No matter what your constraints are, it is wise to consider summer vacations as opportunities to nurture "Future You." Perhaps you will need to work. Perhaps, you'll need to complete additional classes. These added pressures make advance planning even more important. (There is no need to go overboard; you need not plan every minute of your four summers. Nor must you forego fun.)

Here are some summer options to consider:

Conduct Research. Many professors conduct the bulk of their research during the summer, either on campus or in "the field" somewhere. If you can volunteer (i.e., receive no pay) your summer service to an instructor, that can make you an almost impossible-to-turn-down candidate. Whether it's for pay or not, the experience you gain and the relationships you develop can be extremely valuable.

Attend Summer School. There are several potential benefits to taking classes during one or more of the summers.

- If you take one class each summer, it reduces the number of courses you must take during the regular school year, enabling you to perform better in those courses.
- By taking just one class during a summer school session—even if it is on an accelerated schedule, meeting for just six or eight weeks—you can devote all of your study efforts to that one class, without distraction from other classes.

During the regular academic year, Neil struggled for about eight weeks with the third chemistry class (in a four-class sequence) at NYU. Demoralized after failing the first two exams, he decided to drop the class. The following summer, Neil opted to stay at NYU and retake the class, enabling him to focus more on the challenging class. Also, because the class was smaller during summer school, Neil was able to get more help from the professor, earning his highest chemistry grade ever.

- Schools sometimes offer structured summer programs focused on research experiences or interdisciplinary studies. Others offer comprehensive, full-time summer programs that enable you to earn a certificate in recognition of acquiring certain skills, or credit for a minor. At Tulane University, for example, a student can earn a business minor from the Business Minor Summer Institute in ten weeks. Other such programs include:

- ▶ Summer Institute of Environmental Design at UC Berkeley
- ▶ Certificate in International Relations at Columbia University
- ▶ Summer Research Program at MIT
- ▶ Summer program in biomedical sciences at Ohio State

Learn a Foreign Language. At Middlebury Language Schools, for example, you can gain proficiency through their intensive language programs in a wide range of languages, including Arabic, Mandarin, French, and Spanish.

Should You Do a Year Abroad?

Only about five percent of college students spend a full year abroad, but a much larger percentage spend a shorter period—commonly between two and six months—studying at a college outside the U.S. As with summer school, it isn't necessary for you to decide this as soon as you begin college. But it is useful to explore your options as soon as possible.

When Should You Take Your Hardest Classes? Your Easiest Classes? Your Required Classes?

A common—but ill-advised—strategy that many students pursue upon entering college is "to get my requirements out of the way as soon as possible." This sounds good, but usually is not. In a study at Harvard, the vast majority of students taking this "eat my vegetables first" approach said that they regretted that decision.

Similarly, taking all large introductory courses simultaneously leads to reduced satisfaction among students. Researchers have found a strong relationship—reported as a correlation of 0.52—between college satisfaction and the number of low-enrollment courses taken. Students like small classes better.

Another consideration—almost too obvious to require stating—is that there are significant benefits to making sure that you've included something in your schedule each term that you are excited about. (This may help you decide on a major, if you haven't already.) If your academic schedule is filled with required courses, and you are not excited about them, you are pursuing a bad plan.

This all-work-and-no-play mistake is commonly made by pre-med students in particular, who load their schedule with courses in chemistry, physics, and math, rather than building a schedule with better balance between challenging and less-difficult classes, and between required and elective courses.

Which Nonacademic Activities Will You Explore?

When people reflect on their college experiences, their fondest memories are frequently nonacademic. Former First Lady Barbara Bush said, "You'll never regret the time you spent in college talking with friends." Here are some students' best memories looking back on their college years:

- "My best memory of college? When I studied abroad in Perth and Ireland."
- "In a word, *Illuminati* [the school play]."
- "Trying on each other's clothes and laughing until we pee . . ."
- "Club sports were a great alternative to varsity athletics."
- "Something that I had never in a million years expected to be a part of my college experience—rowing for the women's crew team—wound up being the defining aspect of my education."

An important result from a large-scale research study was that students who found meaningful involvement in one or two activities—for up to twenty hours each week—reported significantly greater overall satisfaction with their college experience. In particular, activities that reduce a student's sense of isolation seem to have the greatest value. Options for such involvement include, but are not limited to:

Paid Job. More than half of all college students work, usually seven to twelve hours per week. Surprisingly, such jobs do not reduce grades. Moreover, three-quarters of working students say that their work has a positive effect on their overall college satisfaction. They also report that this work does not have a negative impact on their social experiences. The previous three sentences are unexpected and important enough that you should reread them.

Play a Sport for Your School. For many students, sports are the most intensely bonding and satisfying extracurricular activity, even when intramural.

Participate in the Arts. Among the extracurricular activities associated with the highest student happiness are those in the arts. Students report high satisfaction not just for those positions that serve as training for careers or future work in the arts, but also for activities that are fulfilling and pleasurable in their own right.

Opportunities for arts-related activities abound on campuses:

- Theater—including acting, writing, and producing plays and movies;
- Music—including performing in a band or *a cappella* singing groups;
- Writing—such as for campus publications;
- Politics—including student government and other organizations.

Volunteer. When Alon began college at UC Berkeley, he knew he loved science. "Science is my religion," he liked to say. He had long assumed that he'd become a scientist and "do science" for his career. Toward that end, during his third year he scored a volunteer job in the lab of one of his former biology professors.

It was Alon's dream job. He got to take part in actual research, and he got to see up close what a scientist's daily life was like. And his professor was a thoughtful and valuable mentor for him. For all of these reasons, Alon was surprised to discover that he found the experience mind-numbingly boring!

Was his job a bust? Absolutely not. On the contrary, from this valuable experience Alon determined that although he still loved the *idea* of science and its power to reveal truths about the natural world, he should not continue on his path toward becoming a scientist. His volunteering experience saved Alon the huge effort he would have spent getting into graduate school and learning the lesson only then.

On top of that, from his volunteer lab job, Alon discovered that he loved learning how to program the lab computers and explore the vast data they generated. This knowledge helped guide him toward an extremely successful and creative career in technology (and helped preserve his love of science).

Your Semester-by-Semester Game Plan

Here's a secret that people don't often mention when describing college. You have a *huge* amount of free time. Seriously. Unlike high school, where your every minute is accounted for from about 8am until 3pm, college is almost the opposite.

You'll usually be taking just four or five classes. In most cases, a class will only meet twice a week (Tuesdays and Thursdays) for seventy-five minutes or three times a week (Mondays, Wednesdays, and Fridays) for fifty minutes.

In theory, you could take a full load of classes and only be *in* class for five or six hours on Tuesdays and Thursdays. It's up to you how to spend the rest of your week. (If parents get wind of this, they're going to be confused and angry!)

Additionally, for the most part, nobody from the college is checking up on you. This freedom is nice, but—like the first time someone gets a credit card—without self-discipline, you can get into trouble. "Effective time management" is most often listed by successful college students as central to their success. Among students who fail, "poor time management" ranks near the top of their problems.

Speaking of which . . . On the verge of being dismissed from college for poor performance, Jay stumbled into his first encounter with smart time management. One night at dinner in the cafeteria, his friend Kyle made a proposal. "Hey, we should study together this quarter."

As unremarkable as this study-together suggestion sounds, it turned things around for Jay. He and Kyle decided to go to the BioMed library from 6pm until 10:30pm every night from Sunday through Thursday. (As their reward, they decided that they'd take a thirty-minute break at 8pm and ride their motorcycles around campus.) The role of peers in college is huge; this is a good example of how they can nudge you onto a better track.

Blocking out some dedicated time for study each night became the first step in developing Jay's "Semester-by-Semester Game Plan." You'll need to lay out this game plan at the beginning of each school term. It is primarily about managing your daily time allocation, but you also must build into your schedule blocks of time for investing in your longer-term goals.

In its simplest form, your "Semester-by-Semester Game Plan" can be a daily grid, including all seven days of the week. List all of your regularly scheduled time commitments such as class meetings and work hours. Then "officially" schedule your other needs into the Game Plan. Set yourself up for success by incorporating not just the things you need to do, but also the things you want to do.

- Set aside as many long blocks of time for studying as you can. Studying in short bursts is associated with inefficiency and poor outcomes. At least a few long stretches each week will enable more serious engagement with your lessons.
- Don't schedule study time only for the end of the day; that's when you're more likely to be tired from other activities.
- When scheduling study time, you can reduce wasted "start-up" time by specifying where you will study. You can have two or three or four different places; but for any given study session, know where you're going to do it.
- Schedule group-study periods. Exclusively studying alone is associated with reduced effectiveness.
- Include time for attending your professors' office hours. Don't plan on attending them all—that will make it too tempting (and easy) to deviate from your plan. Focus on attending them early in a term. Professors will be more eager then to give you advice on how to succeed in their class.
- Incorporate a plan for ramping up your preparations for your exams and papers. The week ahead of high-stakes assessments is not like other weeks. You'll need a different schedule.

At least once each term, keep a log of how you spend your time, perhaps in fifteen-minute increments. Be honest. This is the best way to discover whether you are underestimating how long it takes you to spool up your studying. Or to recopy your notes. Or to tend to your messages.

As part of your "Semester-by-Semester Game Plan" determine where you will keep all of your notes: class notes, lab notes, reading notes, exam-study notes. Be organized, methodical, and consistent. Always keep everything organized in one place to reduce time wasted in searching for handouts, syllabi, assignments, etc.

Finally, do not shortchange yourself when it comes to sleep. In a study of the Stanford men's basketball team, the researchers put the Stanford players on a seven-week "sleep extension" program, during which they increased the players' average amount of sleep each night by 110 minutes (almost two hours per night).

The stunning result? Every player's performance (measured during practice) increased significantly for every measure the researchers evaluated. The players' free-throw percentage increased from 79% to 88%. Their three-point field goal percentage increased from 68% to 77%.

Your college success probably doesn't hinge on your basketball shooting accuracy, but it does depend on how much you sleep. The most well-documented and consistent findings across carefully controlled research studies on sleep include:

1. The majority of college students are significantly sleep deprived.
2. Sleep quality and quantity strongly influence learning and academic performance.
3. College students underestimate (spectacularly) the impact of sleep deprivation on their cognitive abilities.

Put another way: You will get better grades if you sleep more. You almost certainly don't believe that this is true. And you are wrong. Now go to bed.

Take Home Messages

1. For some of the most important aspects of college, it is not possible to rush things. Lag time is a nonnegotiable reality. Success requires both a Four-Year Plan and a Semester-by-Semester Plan.

2. As part of the Four-Year Plan, consider how you might spend the summers—travel, internships, or summer school.

3. Participate in two or three significant extracurricular activities.

4. Structure your academic schedule to take a mix of classes each term. Rather than bulking up on large intro classes and/or required courses, take at least one small, fun class each term.

5. In college, you can do whatever is necessary to not fail. Or you can do everything that is possible to excel. Establishing a realistic Semester-by-Semester Game Plan as well as making time for study, play, and sleep will help you excel.

PLANNING SEMESTER AND LIFE GOALS

*"Omphaloskepsis"—contemplation of one's
navel as an aid to meditation.*

When we (Jay and Terry) were in graduate school, we served as advisors to Harvard college students. One spring, a soon-to-be-graduating senior, Prishna, asked us for career advice: "I can't decide if I want to go to medical school or to graduate school in physics. What do you suggest?"

We responded, "Graduation is in two months, what have you done to investigate these two career paths?" Prishna replied, "I have been spending a lot of time in my room thinking very hard about which of the two alternatives would be better."

In other words, Prishna had been engaged in omphaloskepsis—staring at her belly button. And while some people with hectic lives might gain some perspective from a bout of navel gazing, in Prishna's case, omphaloskepsis until two months before graduation was probably not the wisest use of time.

What is a more productive approach when you are undecided between two options? The answer is to aggressively explore both.

Prishna's approach was particularly perplexing because Harvard uses a housing system designed to help students learn about myriad careers. Each of the twelve Harvard residential "houses" includes at least one tenured professor and a dozen or more graduate students from across a variety of fields. These advisors live in the same buildings as the college students and eat in the same cafeteria.

Harvard commits to this huge expenditure for live-in advisors so that the undergraduates have access to a rich resource of knowledge, wisdom, and experience. When a student has a need, Harvard's hope is that someone with excellent qualifications is already nearby to help.

Prishna lived on the third floor, and on the second floor—almost directly below her—lived Mei, a PhD student in physics at Harvard. Prishna could have begun meaningful exploration of one of her preferred careers in less than a minute.

In most cases, it takes more than a minute to begin learning about future careers. Nevertheless, there are some easy first steps that anyone can—and should—take, including going to academic and career counselors and contacting people in the profession and asking to meet them. Earlier in this book, we met Florian who wanted to be a surgeon until the day he shadowed a surgeon and saw the reality of the job. That sort of just-in-time lesson is hugely valuable.

———

What will you accomplish in college and make of your life? Our goal is to help you get the best possible outcomes. The specific details of these best outcomes, though, differ hugely from one person to the next. Some want to create something original—a novel, a movie, a piece of music, a software application. Others seek to build a rich social world. For still others, they seek to bring about change in the world. And for many, it is some combination of these and other outcomes.

As with any important and complex endeavor, putting together your list of goals is easier if you divide the project into smaller, more manageable chunks. For starters, there are several different aspects of your life for which you'll want to establish goals: your academic work, your career progress, health and fitness, and finances.

There are different time frames for which you'll have goals, too. You may ultimately want to live near the beach. But that shouldn't necessarily preclude you from moving somewhere far from the beach for your dream summer internship. Some of your goals are part of a longer game.

Reflecting on how to weigh short-term versus long-term goals when they seem to conflict is an ongoing—and fun—part of living an examined life.

The following might serve as a useful framework:

Academic work
- explore options and decide on a major
- develop effective study habits
- achieve some academic performance goals (Dean's list? No C's?)

Career progress
- develop a relationship with a mentor
- narrow the list of potential job areas you'd like to explore
- secure an internship in a field you might be interested in
- establish a long record (more than a year) as a reliable, exemplary worker in a job

■ craft a resume and personal website for advancing your career

Fitness

■ develop and stick to a regular fitness program
■ achieve expertise in a sport or fitness activity (running, yoga, weightlifting, etc.)
■ reach and maintain a desired body weight/composition

Finances

■ establish a personal budget
■ maintain a consistent rate of savings
■ develop and adhere to a realistic plan of debt reduction
■ investigate long-term strategies/philosophies of financial management

Personal goals

■ read works of literature (for pleasure!)
■ identify and explore personal projects that interest you, perhaps:
  ▶ improve your skills in photography or painting or ping-pong or cooking or DJ'ing
  ▶ produce items of value for your friends, your family, and/or yourself—scrapbooking, collections of photos, traditional letters
  ▶ restore and enjoy an old car or bike or other collectible item
  ▶ master a software application that you'll likely use in the future
■ organize social events—a party or a regular game night or a day trip somewhere (hiking? beach? restaurant?)
■ explore and learn about the city in which you live and beyond; identify places of interest off the beaten track (e.g., museums, art galleries, trails, neighborhoods)

Start with this: What are your top goals in college right now? Write down the top three for your academic life, your social life, and your work life. We suggest that you develop a small number of high priorities for each area of your life. As you are developing your lists, don't lose sight of this guiding principle:

This. Should. Be. Fun.

Think about it: you are deciding who you want to be and what you want to do in (and with) your life. What could be more fun than that? No one's opinion matters more than your own about what should be on your list. Your parents get to live their lives; they don't get to live your life, too. Same goes for your advisors and friends.

Don't worry about getting things just right at the outset. Think of your Goal Lists as living entities, growing and changing as necessary. They can encompass something as complex as your career exploration, or they can articulate simple guiding principles for a summer adventure, which was once the case for Terry.

In establishing his goals for a summer he was spending in Uganda at a chimpanzee research station, Terry settled on just three priorities:

1. Stay alive.
2. Keep his boss happy.
3. Have fun.

This clear road map of priorities helped focus and streamline Terry's decision-making. For example, how should Terry travel the 200 miles from the airport in Kampala to the research site in the western part of the country? The possibilities were: a) take a bus for $5, b) ride in a shared van for $20, or c) hire a private car for $250. Money was tight and taking a car would mean many sacrifices during the summer.

Mindful of achieving goal #1 (stay alive), however, Terry took a significant part of his budget and arranged for a private car. He was careful to take down the license plate number, and show the driver that he was sending a message to his family with the plate number. The point was to make sure the driver knew there would be repercussions for kidnapping or murder.

That same summer, two other researchers took the lower cost routes from Kampala. One chose the $5 bus and, disastrously, was drugged by a fellow passenger who had put sleeping potion in a cake and then offered the cake to the researcher. The researcher awoke to discover that he had been robbed of all his money and valuables (including an expensive camera necessary for his work).

The other researcher chose the $20 shared van option. Such overloaded vans careen around the roads, however, in a high-risk race to make the most money in the least amount of time. This particular van got into a terrible accident and another passenger in the van was killed in the crash. The researcher was okay (and was not robbed). But some horrible images will remain with him for the rest of his life.

Terry arrived much poorer but safe after his private drive, at least in part because he made a decision that was aligned with his Goal List.

In chapter 1, Terry listed some of the jobs he has held. They include busboy, lawnmower, short-order cook, slaughterhouse worker, lifeguard, swim instructor, computer programmer, college professor, construction worker, economist, portfolio manager, Marine Corps tank driver, and research scientist.

When considering his career path, Terry's main self-critique is that he wandered for too long, taking an unnecessarily circuitous route. Eventually, he did land some jobs that he liked—computer programmer, portfolio manager, economist, and college professor—but he feels he could have gotten there sooner.

Just a few years ago, and more than halfway through his working years, Terry revisited the Myers-Briggs personality test, which he had first taken in the 1980s. The Myers-Briggs assessment is grounded in the work of Carl Jung, a psychoanalyst who was a student of Sigmund Freud.

The caricature of Freud is that adult personality characteristics are driven by childhood experiences. For example, a drill instructor in the movie *Full Metal Jacket* screams at a struggling new recruit, "What's the matter, didn't mommy and daddy show you enough love?"

Such Freudian observations assume that adult personalities are created by childhood experiences. In contrast, Jung rejected the notion that it is only life experiences that impact personality. Instead, he believed that people are born with some personality proclivities.

These innate tendencies are then modified by the events of your life (including how you got along with your mother and father). From this perspective, your personality reflects much more than the parenting style in your childhood home. Far from it. (Anyone with at least one sibling has seen this first-hand.)

Researchers Isabel Myers and her mother Katharine Briggs sought to measure personality and make Jung's views actionable. Their "Myers-Briggs" test places people into one of sixteen categories based on a self-assessment questionnaire evaluating dimensions.

E or I	–	Extravert	or	Introvert
N or S	–	Intuitive	or	Sensing
F or T	–	Feeling	or	Thinking
P or J	–	Perception	or	Judging

For those who enjoy such questionnaires and the self-reflection they require, the process can be fun. For example, Terry is an INTP, sometimes called, 'The Logician.' Here is one description of such a person:

INTPs live in the world of theoretical possibilities. They see everything in terms of how it could be improved, or what it could be turned into. They live primarily inside their own minds, having the ability to analyze difficult problems, identify patterns, and come up with logical explanations. They seek clarity in everything and are therefore driven to build knowledge.

What does 'The Logician' have to do with career choices? Research has linked Myers-Briggs personality types to careers that are likely to be satisfying. After Terry had spent decades searching for a career, a friend showed Terry a website that listed the best jobs for each Myers-Briggs personality type. The list suggested the following careers for Terry's personality type:

- computer programmer
- portfolio manager
- economist
- college professor
- wealth management

Four of these five are exactly the careers that Terry discovered and the fifth, wealth management, is something he has considered. In short, Myers-Briggs and thirty minutes might have reduced the twenty or so years that Terry spent flailing.

Is the lesson that we should all pick jobs consistent with our Myers-Briggs personality types? No. But taking a small amount of time to assess yourself is probably time well spent. Most college career or advising centers will administer personality tests including Myers-Briggs for free. We should not forget that career success requires spending time on self-examination as well as identifying external opportunities.

Would you like a job that paid over $150,000 per year, with significant flexibility in hours? Sleep late one day a week and roll into work at 1pm. Go surfing at sunset on another day. High pay, flexible hours, and some social status. Sounds great. Right?

What if this $150,000 job with flexibility was being a dentist? A life spent amidst halitosis, plaque, and pain. A recent study noted that dentists—who do earn an average of $150K—had among the worst fit between their job requirements and their personalities.

What are the most sought-after careers among young people? Pop star and professional athlete rank near the top. Even these appealing fields, however, have attributes that can be challenging. Many such entertainers, for example, are on the road for months at a time each year. Some people might love this travel, but others might prefer to have a family and spend more time at home.

Not only do athletes travel almost continuously, they also face physical dangers. In 2017, 291 NFL players suffered concussions. There are just 1,696 professional football players, so close to twenty percent suffered concussions just in that one year!

Former Chicago Bears player Dave Duerson committed suicide in 2011. In his suicide note, he asked that his brain be donated for study to look for concussion-related damage. Similarly, San Diego Charger and New England Patriot star Junior Seau committed suicide in 2013; Seau's family commissioned a study, which reported that he had degenerative brain disease. The NFL is being sued for concussion-related brain damage by more than a thousand former players.

We still suspect that being a rock star or professional athlete might be awesome. The point, however, is that there is no one perfect job for all people. Finding the right fit requires persistent investigation both of oneself and of different career characteristics.

There is a Taoist story, "Maybe," that goes as follows:

A rich man comes to town and gives a horse to a farmer. Upon hearing the news, the farmer's neighbors say, "How wonderful."

"Maybe," the farmer replies.

The following day, the farmer's son falls off the horse, and breaks his leg. The neighbors come to offer their sympathy on his misfortune. "How terrible," they say.

"Maybe," answers the farmer.

The day after, military officials come to the village to draft young men into the army. Seeing that the son's leg is broken, they pass him by. The neighbors congratulated the farmer on how well things had turned out. "Wonderful news!"

"Maybe," says the farmer.

When we judge the success of careers, we should keep 'maybe' in mind. Let's look at the case of another young student, named Luca, who lived in the same community with Terry, Jay, and Prishna.

Luca had many interesting characteristics, including some strong preferences and aversions. First, he absolutely hated to fly. Second, he loved music and sports more than anything. In fact, Luca spent significant time and money travelling by bus (never planes!) to attend concerts.

When asked about interviewing for jobs as a college senior, Luca demurred. "Corporations are not my thing. I'd have to wear a suit, and probably fly. I like my sports and my concerts." Two years after graduating from Harvard, Luca was living back at home with his mother in Florida.

Was Luca a success? One might be tempted to say that he was not a success; the Taoist view leads us to "maybe."

After a few years of struggling and searching, Luca obtained his dream job. He was paid to watch and write about sports. Specifically, his job was to cover NASCAR for ESPN. The beauty of NASCAR, for a person who hates to fly, is that all the competitions are on weekends so it is possible to travel between events without flying.

Consider another "maybe failure" story. In 1932, a sixty-five-year-old woman was financially destitute. She had had two children, one of whom died young. Her husband had been a charismatic, athletic young man, but became permanently paralyzed soon after their wedding. Additionally, the woman's own childhood had been punctuated by tragedies, and she lived most of her life in poverty and debt. At sixty-five, she was likely near the end of her life, broke, and with no obvious path forward.

On their own, these facts might suggest that the woman's life was a failure. At sixty-five, however, she was just getting started. The woman was Laura Ingalls Wilder, and 1932 was when she began publishing the autobiographical *Little House on the Prairie* books that have been spectacularly popular.

For comparison, the best-selling book in the history of the world, other than religious texts, is *The Lord of the Rings*, having sold around 150 million copies. Collectively, the Harry Potter books are closing in on 500 million copies sold. The books in the Little House series together have sold between 50 and 100 million copies. This makes Laura Ingalls Wilder one of history's most successful writers.

How did Laura come to write such popular books? Interestingly, tragedy and failure played central roles. Here are but a few incidents in her life that no one would willingly choose to endure.

Laura's sister Mary went blind as a child. Consequently, Laura became Mary's eyes, sitting next to her sister for hours describing the world. This continual descriptive effort played an important role in Laura remembering so many details of their lives, and in developing her ability to describe events.

Beyond its level of detail, Laura's writing derives much of its power from its simple, emotion-free language—the sort of language that would be helpful for a blind sister. The first line of the first book is, "Once upon a time, sixty years ago, a little girl lived in the Big Woods of Wisconsin, in a little gray house made of logs."

Entitled *Little House on the Prairie*, Wilder's third book begins, "A long time ago . . . Pa and Ma and Mary and Laura and Baby Carrie left their little house in the Big Woods of Wisconsin. They drove away and left it lonely and empty in the clearing among the big trees, and they never saw that little house again."

This opening wasn't something Laura conjured from thin air. It happened that Laura's father, Charles Ingalls, was disastrously inept when it came to money and planning. These traits repeatedly led to difficulties. In one case not covered in the Little House books, the family had to flee a town before dawn, leaving behind a mountain of unpaid debt.

The third book in the series chronicles a similar situation, however. The Ingalls family built a log house on a prairie. They succeeded in planting crops even in the face of numerous hardships—Pa falling down the well, the family getting malaria, and a raging prairie fire.

As the year comes to an end, however, Pa tells Ma they must move because the U.S. Army is going to evict them from the lands where they have built the home. The entire series is named after this "snug log house," yet it was occupied by the Ingalls family for just a few months because Laura's father did not secure the rights to the property before construction.

There are many other examples where apparent misfortune led to something positive for Laura Ingalls Wilder. In fact, it was out of desperation that she wrote the books in the first place. Laura and her husband, Almanzo, had been forced to sell their farming properties because of crop losses, a fire that destroyed their house, and the onset of Almanzo's paralysis. For tens of millions of readers, as well as for Laura, it could almost be considered fortunate that she and Almanzo did not find success in farming.

We do not know where events in life will take us, and we should not evaluate ourselves or others prematurely. Even at sixty-five, it was too early to judge Laura Ingalls Wilder's life and career.

Take Home Messages

1. When deciding between multiple career options, investigate as many as possible simultaneously. Valuable information that you need is available out in the world. Leave your room and actively work to learn about your options.

2. Spend time (and have fun) developing Goal Lists for each area of your life. These goals should describe the outcomes that you want to achieve.

3. The right job fits into the personality of the person. People are wildly different in likes and dislikes. Investigate yourself as well as the world.

4. Do not judge yourself or others prematurely. Strive to improve your situation and help others. Do not give up because you have not succeeded yet.

PLANNING DAILY AND WEEKLY GOALS

After long days working in the lab, Jay often would stop by Terry's room for a visit. (We lived in the same building during graduate school.) One particular day, Terry seemed frustrated and unhappy with his day. So Jay asked, "What did you do today?"

"I bought some pants."

Indeed, there were half a dozen pairs of pants on the bed. "That seems reasonable. What's the problem?"

Terry then opened the computer file with his day's "To-do List." On it, Jay could see a handful of items. One of these was "Buy pants," with a check mark next to it. Unfortunately, only a few other items had been checked off. The item at the top of the list, unchecked, was "Write PhD dissertation."

"Every day, I'm busy all day—usually occupied with a million tasks, like buying pants," Terry explained. "Before I get to 'Write dissertation,' I run out of time and energy."

In this chapter we explore how you can best structure your days and weeks to achieve the outcomes you decide that you want.

The pathway to productivity first requires identifying and prioritizing your goals. We've discussed these important processes in the preceding chapter. Once you have done this, you can set yourself up for success by organizing your efforts into Task Lists—aligned with your goals—that facilitate continuous and significant productivity.

Step 1: Identify, Categorize, and Prioritize Your Goals

President Jimmy Carter is often ranked among the least effective U.S. presidents. This may be, in part, a result of his penchant for micromanaging and spending too much time on petty details.

According to one of Carter's speechwriters, for example, it was necessary to go through the president to schedule time on the White House tennis court. Similarly, President Carter spent many hours designing the uniforms for some of the White House staff, ruminating, for example, on the finish of the buttons. Should the buttons be shiny or brushed?

Meanwhile, the country suffered through a period of high inflation, high unemployment, and an oil crisis, while Iran held fifty-two Americans hostage for more than a year. (It is unclear whether President Carter also bought pants during this period, but we suspect that he did.)

How can you avoid these mistakes? First, it's essential to recognize that you are unlikely to make significant progress toward your goals if you don't know what those goals are. And second, you must come to terms with the disappointing reality that, like President Carter, you don't have an unlimited amount of time and can't do everything. Consequently, you must prioritize your goals.

Which of President Carter's tasks would have been the least disastrous if left undone? He probably could have survived (and maybe been reelected) even if twenty people showed up to play tennis at the exact same time one Saturday morning. But failing to resolve the issues that led to hour-long waits at gas stations for millions of people, on the other hand, had calamitous consequences for his political success.

Step 2: Build Your To-Do Lists with the Tasks Necessary for Achieving Your Goals

At a birthday party several years ago, Jay first met his good friend, Tannaz. In the midst of telling a story about her work, Tannaz mentioned that, although she liked her job as a computer programmer, her real dream was to be a food writer.

Curious, Jay asked, "When did you last actually write about food?" Tannaz's reply was perfect: "This morning. I wrote about food this morning. I have a food blog and wrote a story for it, called 'Sage Wine and Flowers.'"

It's fun and easy to dwell on the excitement of our goals, embellishing and dreaming about them. But we'd be wise to take a lesson from Tannaz. Our goals become infinitely more likely to turn into realities if we are able to translate them to "Task Lists." Specifically, we need to determine all the tasks that align with our goals, prioritize them, and complete them.

Tasks are related to goals, but they are not the same. Tasks are better thought of as the means to an end. Your goals are the outcomes you desire, while your tasks should be the specific things that you can do, measure, and definitively complete. Accomplishing them moves you closer to achieving your goals.

Your goals might include:

- Improve your cooking skills.
- Lose weight.
- Get better grades.

These items are laudable goals, but they are too general and nebulous to guide your behavior at this exact moment. Still, they should guide you in creating Task Lists filled with action items closely aligned with your goals. For example:

- Find a new recipe each week and make it.
- Use intermittent fasting; do not eat before noon or after 8pm.
- Recopy class notes each day and write twelve questions and detailed answers based on each lecture.

Keep in mind that each Task List item must be something that you can—with no uncertainty—answer with a yes or no as to whether you have completed it. There can be no gray area.

Your Task Lists should guide you in deciding how to spend the minutes and hours of your days. This sounds trivially straightforward and simple. For a variety of reasons, however, it is rarely as easy as it might seem.

That is why even smart, accomplished people can stumble in their efforts to attain their goals. Pants-buying Terry has a PhD from Harvard. Tennis-court scheduler Jimmy Carter was elected to the most powerful leadership position in the world. Yet they both struggled in advancing toward their goals.

Why? The problem stems from our human nature. As the products of evolution, humans all have brains with some quirks that can lead to inactivity or pants-buying.

To clarify this idea, let's take a brief *BioBreak* for a primer on how we are built and what motivates us. Stay with us because the answer has important implications for every aspect of our lives—including how we should create our Task Lists and why we sometimes struggle to maximize our productivity.

BioBreak: How Is Our Brain Built and What Motivates Us?

When Jay was about ten years old, riding his bike one day he found a twenty-dollar bill. Imagining all of the glorious possibilities afforded by this money made Jay ridiculously happy. But he also was perplexed.

Finding the money made him happier, but contemplating his friends and their families he sensed that, for the most part, those who were richer weren't necessarily happier than those with less. It felt like an Escher optical illusion drawing: walking up steps but ending up in the same place.

It took several decades for Jay to understand how this apparent paradox could be resolved. It required a change in perspective.

Consider some emotions: jealousy, anger, guilt. Where do they come from? What is their purpose? You'll likely know from your own experiences with these brain states that they generally cause you to alter your behavior.

Feeling desire for another person, a potential partner, what do you do? You try to be the best version of yourself around them, to attract them to you. Feeling anger—perhaps about some unfair treatment? You again alter your behavior—perhaps to punish someone else and to secure a better outcome for yourself. Our genes have built us to nudge ourselves subconsciously toward behaviors that benefit them.

Happiness, too, works in this way. Striving toward our goals activates reward centers in our brain, causing us to experience pleasure. We are motivated by that sensation of happiness, but that's just the carrot that incentivizes us to act in ways that further our genes' interests.

There are some unexpected consequences of being built with a motivation-and-reward system in which success is measured by relative performance. Our genes nudge us toward improvement, not absolute levels of achievement. This subtle distinction is responsible for the fact that emotions are less permanent than they feel.

We imagine that achieving our goals will make us happy; that anticipation motivates us to work toward them. We believe catastrophic events will forever preclude happiness and so take great care to avoid them. In both cases, we are wrong. We experience happiness when we are making progress toward our goals. And we evaluate our progress by comparing where we are at any point in time with where we were previously and where we expected to be.

Back to ten-year-old Jay's paradox. Why is it that finding twenty dollars makes us happier, but rich people seem no happier than poor? This unexpected event dramatically highlighted a change in Jay's situation. Change like that is what generates happiness.

Here's a wacky research study (by a Nobel Prize winner) that only makes sense with this evolutionary perspective on happiness. Researchers studied approximately 700 patients undergoing colonoscopies, an extremely unpleasant medical procedure.

Half of the patients endured the regular twenty-minute colonoscopy. The other half underwent the regular colonoscopy, *plus* an extended procedure. Following the twenty-minute colonoscopy, the tip of the colonoscope remained inside the patient for five additional minutes, but in a way that made these five minutes progressively less painful than the previous twenty minutes.

Which patients do you think ranked their experience as more unpleasant: those experiencing twenty painful minutes or those experiencing twenty painful minutes *plus* five additional minutes of pain that was slightly less intense?

Those whose colonoscopy lasted longer but ended with slight improvement overwhelmingly ranked the entire experience as less unpleasant. Not only that, but they also were forty percent more likely to return for a follow-up visit. We are built to experience happiness when we are experiencing improvement in our situation. This sheds light on some silly To-Do List practices, as we'll see.

Step 2.1: Tweak Your Task Lists with an Eye to Ensuring Productivity

With this biological perspective on what happiness is, it's easier now to see why "Buy pants" was a more appealing task for Terry than "Write dissertation." He gets pleasure from checking something off his list; he's making progress! And buying pants takes much less effort than would be required to write his dissertation.

Have you ever put something on your list that you already did, and then checked it off? Have you ever put something on your list that you would absolutely do, regardless of whether it was on the list or not? "Eat lunch." Or perhaps, "Take shower."

As ridiculous as this seems, it highlights an important tactic for setting yourself up for success when it comes to building Task Lists:

- Break down your tasks into manageable items that make it easy to see progress.

In other words, replace, "Write dissertation" with items that are less daunting: "Decide on four dissertation chapter titles."

"Write first line of Chapter 1." "Sketch a graph with the most important data from the first experiment." And go from there.

The poet Ovid was onto something when he wrote, *Adde parvum parvo magnus acervus erit*—"By adding little to little there will be a great heap."

In addition to spending time developing items that are manageable in scope, consider their relative importance. Jim Koch is the multimillionaire founder of the Sam Adams beer company. He was a pioneer in launching smaller label, craft beers and his company has become a massive success.

Early in his career, Jim received a phone call from his father. "What are you doing today, son?" Jim answered that he was spending the day selecting computers for his new company, an important concern. The father said, "Hang up the phone, get in your car, and go sell some beer."

At the time of this phone call, Sam Adams beer had won several high-profile beer tasting competitions, but sales were slow. Partly in response to his father's advice, the founder began devoting more of his time to personally driving to bars and liquor stores, where he made his sales pitch. Eventually, these pitches added up to the juggernaut we see today.

Had we asked Jim Koch his priorities on the day his father called, he would have answered: 1. Sales, 2. Sales, and 3. Sales. Is the message here that sales are always most important or that father always knows best? No. The message is that success requires focus on the most important issues.

At the end of any week, you should be able to make a chart of how you have spent your hours. Success requires that your allocation of time aligns with your goals. Jim Koch said his highest priority was selling beer, but his behavior said that buying computers was more important. If you spend your time watching TV, your highest priority is TV, regardless of your stated goals.

Sometimes an inability to work on priorities is a red flag signaling a need for change. Consider the story of a secretary who was chastised repeatedly for neglecting her official tasks, and instead spent her time writing stories. In this case, the fired secretary was J.K. Rowling and her writing led her to create the world of Harry Potter.

Perhaps your family really wants you to be an engineer, and you have taken all the right steps on the path to becoming an engineer. However, you find that you are unable to spend time on your engineering studies. Your motivational issue might be caused by having the wrong goals rather than a lack of discipline.

None of this is easy. Success requires hard, persistent work that often is boring. Are you the next J.K. Rowling? Possibly. Regardless, our advice here is to work hard toward your stated goals, and to monitor the alignment between your goals and your effort.

If you are writing Harry Potter when you should be doing calculus, perhaps you should become a writer. If, on the other hand, you are binge-watching entire seasons of TV shows or getting drunk regularly, a deeper exploration of your goals and motivations, rather than a simple change of major, may be necessary.

Finally, in addition to developing action items that are doable and appropriately ranked according to their relative importance, make sure that your integration of Task Lists into your daily work process enhances your productivity.

In his job at UCLA, Jay found himself feeling like he was spinning his wheels. He'd work hard all day, completing tasks and checking things off his daily productivity list. But each day, he also was adding new items to the list, such as when students requested recommendation letters or colleagues invited him to collaborate on research projects.

Jay might start the day with twenty items on the list and, over the course of the day, complete twenty tasks. But because he'd also have added another twenty items, the list never got shorter. He'd go home at the end of the day and, rather than feeling happy and productive, he felt like he had been hurled off a treadmill at the same place he got on. The list always won.

Now each day Jay separates out "Today's List," and doesn't allow himself to add to it. New items can only be placed on the "Future Items" list. And as the day proceeds, he works through his list until everything is done. At the end of the day, he still has checked off about twenty items. But he feels satisfaction from completing the list.

It's just a trick, yet it's surprisingly effective at manipulating the pleasure centers in his brain to improve morale. You'll no longer see Jay shuffling slowly to the parking lot, defeated by The List. Now you can see him skipping out to his car with a smile on his face.

Because we all have different goals and different work habits and preferences, it's important to build in flexibility to your productivity processes. Amazon, for example, has made many big changes over the years. In the early days, if a customer wrote down a negative number for quantity, Amazon would pay the customer. Ordering "negative five" copies of *Mean Genes* at twenty dollars per copy, led to the customer getting paid $100 by Amazon. Founder Jeff Bezos quipped that "presumably we then waited for the customer to ship us the books."

Just as Amazon made adjustments, so will you in your productivity plans. Sadly, there is no alternative to the hard work of recording your outcomes, evaluating where you succeeded and where you fell short in attaining your goals, and then changing your goals and/or your behavior. A small silver lining is that this means it is more important to start *now* than to get hung up devising the best process.

Jay's first introduction to list-making came in his third year of college. He noticed that each night, his roommate Pat jotted down five or six tasks for the following day, using a tiny scrap of paper he placed next to his bed. At the end of the day, he'd put that day's list into a Tupperware tub.

Every so often, Pat would dig through the container to look at what he had been accomplishing (and which tasks languished, appearing on the lists for many days). Pat's methods weren't pretty, but they were dramatically more effective than the haphazard ways that Jay stumbled through those days.

Start with a few simple lists. Explore different ways of managing them. There are many apps designed to help you with your productivity management. But don't worry too much about which one you choose, if any.

Postscript: You: 2.0, 2.1, 3.0 . . .

Consider the existing you as "You 1.0." Think about what you like about yourself and what you would like to change. Now envisage "You 2.0"—a better version of yourself that retains your core strengths, but with some new and improved attributes.

Changing oneself is not easy. Every microscopic improvement requires effort and sacrifice. But the results can include not just better outcomes, but also happiness.

Start small. Take one trivial aspect of your life and try to make a change. For example, if you are often rushed in the morning, try to leave earlier. To make this change requires you first to measure your current behavior. Record the time of departure for one month, then try to leave, say, five minutes earlier on average. Record your time for the next month. Now compare.

Then consider larger changes. Change your diet to eat higher quality foods. Move your grade point average up by half a grade. Become a better friend. A big change such as earning better grades might be ten or a hundred times harder than leaving five minutes earlier every day. But in achieving small successes, you can develop and refine processes for feedback and revision that will help with the larger challenges.

There's no getting around it. Becoming a new and better you will be hard. Just don't lose sight of the fact that improvement is both possible and necessary for success. You 2.0 is inside, ready to emerge.

Take Home Messages

1. Task Lists identify the specific things you must do to achieve your goals. In addition to being aligned with your goals, each item must be something that you can do, measure, and definitively complete.

2. Emotions are the products of evolution. They exist to alter our behavior, nudging us toward behaviors that benefit our genes. As a consequence, absolute levels of achievement have little effect on happiness. Rather, we love making progress toward our goals.

3. Structure your Task Lists—and, consequently, the days and weeks of your life—with an eye toward perpetually making progress.

4. Keep organized records and revisit your past lists. Identify your successes and failures. Evaluate the effectiveness of your tactics and revise them when necessary.

5. You can become a different and better person. Achieving the "new you" requires persistent, informed, costly effort. Take time to define your priorities, focus your effort on those priorities, measure your progress, and refine your behavior.

ACHIEVING GOALS:
HOW TO INTERACT EFFECTIVELY
AND GET STUFF THAT YOU NEED

IN CHOOSING YOUR COURSES SEEK GREAT TEACHERS

The right teacher can change your life for the better. The wrong teacher can bore you, dissuade you from taking a productive path, and make college seem worthless.

Emily Blunt, the actress, had a teacher who changed her life. As a child, Emily had a terrible stutter. She describes her life then as miserable. She didn't want to speak, didn't participate in class, and was at odds with her parents about her path forward. Blunt said that pronouncing her own vowel-filled name was "hell," and that her stutter was like a "straitjacket."

A caring teacher changed Blunt's life forever with a seemingly ridiculous suggestion: try out for the school play. Blunt's teacher, however, genuinely was concerned for her and had spent time observing young Emily. The teacher saw that Blunt would sometimes do impressions for her friends or speak in the voice of another person. In those situations, the stutter somehow disappeared!

The rest is history. Blunt became a movie star, with a successful career and personal life. And it all started because she had one amazing teacher. The wrong teacher, on the other hand, can produce lasting damage.

Fortunately, in college, students have considerable control when it comes to selecting their instructors.

In this chapter, we explore how to make wise use of this control. Keep in mind, of course, that while our focus here is on finding the best teachers for you, numerous aspects of course selection are important and should all be taken into consideration.

———————

Having made it through many years of schooling already, you know—in a qualitative sense—that teachers vary tremendously. But let's look at some data to get a more quantitative perspective on how this can matter to you.

At one top ten university, each term there are three offerings of an introductory biology class (each with 200–300 students). Each offering is taught by a different instructor, but they all use a common exam. This makes it possible to estimate how much student performance depends on the instructor.

Does teacher quality matter? Hugely! Grades are not the only measure of teacher effectiveness—more on this in a bit—but across the common exam questions the average score of students having Professor 3 was four percentage points higher than for those with Professor 1. Because final grades in this class are based on a straight scale, four percentage points represented close to half a grade. That is enough to boost everyone, for example, from B+ to A–.

The fact that students learn more and get better grades from good teachers is not news. More than fifty years ago, leading researchers produced a seminal 746-page report filled with empirical evidence about what works and what doesn't work in education. One of the key conclusions of the report is that teacher quality has a very large effect on student performance. In fact, teacher quality mattered more than a school's overall quality or the curriculum.

In other words, it's not enough to choose the right school. Once you get there, you need to choose instructors wisely. There's more: robust evidence documents that the benefits of high teacher quality extend beyond grades, including improved employment outcomes and higher salaries.

So which professors should you take? This would be a very short chapter if we could simply advise you to "seek great teachers." But it rarely comes down to "good" versus "bad" teachers. It's more complicated than that. The situation is analogous with buying a car. It's useless to just ask someone, "Which car should I buy?" How could they possibly answer you? "Seek great cars" wouldn't be wrong. But it wouldn't help either.

Consumer Reports magazine declared the Toyota Prius as the "most reliable car for 2021." Is that going to work for you if you are a carpenter and need to haul a table-saw and sheets of plywood? *The Robb Report* selected the Lamborghini Huracán as "Car of the Year 2020." Will its lack of a back seat be problematic when you need to drive your kids to school? *Car and Driver* featured the BMW 8-series Gran Coupe in its "Most beautiful cars of 2020" roundup. Sticker price? About $100,000.

As with cars, there isn't just one measure by which all teachers can be compared and ranked. Educational researchers struggle with the challenge of "teacher quality," in part because it comprises several distinct elements. Effective instructors:

- create and use engaging learning opportunities;
- guide students in ways that help them learn;
- evaluate and monitor learning using multiple sources of evidence; and

- contribute to positive academic attitudes and outcomes (short- and long-term).

These skills and techniques require numerous other characteristics, including having high expectations and utilizing effective goal-setting, content expertise, flexibility, strong communication skills, respect for and interest in students, and collaboration with other scholars and instructors.

What then makes a great teacher? Given the multiple dimensions of teaching, simple evaluation on one dimension is not possible and doesn't even make sense. There is no such thing as a "best teacher."

And yet you still must "seek great teachers" if you are to get the best outcomes in college. In order to know how to do that, however, you must first figure out what *you* are looking for. Until you think about this in a methodical fashion, you may not actually know what you're looking for. Moreover, what you are looking for may not be the same from year to year or even course to course.

Is the course you are investigating within your major or is it a general education course? Have you selected a major or are you exploring? Might you benefit from venturing out beyond your comfort zone? Could you use a break from classes closely related to your major? Have you sought out courses that might help you improve your critical thinking and reasoning skills? These questions matter; they'll help you determine whether you are looking for a "great" two-seat convertible or a "great" SUV with four-wheel drive.

Think of your "great teacher search algorithm" as a dynamic entity. It depends on the specifics of the situation, and you should always be making it better. Sample. Evaluate. Revise.

So now you have a sense of the varied elements of teacher quality and you've developed an idea of what you want and need. What's next? Because no one source of information about teachers is perfect or sufficient, you must utilize multiple sources in order to find the best teacher for you.

■ *Consult teacher evaluations.*

In one of the most widely cited papers on this topic, researcher Howard Wachtel summarized: "after nearly seven decades of research on the use of student evaluations of teaching effectiveness, it can safely be stated that the majority of researchers believe that student ratings are a valid, reliable, and worthwhile means of evaluating teaching."

As we discuss further in the next section, however, evaluations must be interpreted with caution. Typically, you have little information about the student evaluators' motivations and interests in the course, their prior knowledge, or their goals in taking the class. These influence the extent to which their evaluations are relevant to your specific needs.

■ *Ask your friends.*

Opinions and information from your friends can be useful, particularly to the extent that they have insights into your interests, motivations, and abilities. But again, remember that you can't simply ask them, "What car should I buy?"

Rather, get as much context as possible with their thoughts and opinions. This will help you determine whether their recommendations have value for you. Ask specific questions: Which features of Instructor A's teaching were most valuable for you? Which were the least valuable? Why? What were you looking for from the class?

Is it relevant to know that they were looking for an easy class with few time commitments when you are seeking a course with field trips and independent research opportunities? Of course.

- *Sit in on a class or watch a recording of one.*
  Is there much student-teacher interaction? Are the students engaged? Can you detect other indicators that the instructor's methods will resonate with you?

- *Contact the professor.*

- *Review the syllabus beforehand.*

- *Explore the instructor's social media.*

- *Seek out relevant student organizations.*
  Investigate if there are any clubs or student groups related to the instructor's field. Through these organizations, you can meet experienced students who are likely to share some of your goals and needs relating to course and instructor selection.

Because they typically represent the most significant factor influencing instructor selection, student evaluations of teachers warrant a closer look.

Is there a clear relationship between instructor ratings and student outcomes? Research evidence paints a nuanced picture. Consider these two academic studies. Both employed the same core methodology: Student knowledge was tested before and after a class to measure what they learned during the course. The increases in scores during the course were then compared, evaluating a variety of variables including instructor experience and student ratings.

In 2009, Professors Oreopoulos and Hoffmann published *Professor Qualities and Student Achievement*. They reported that, "We find that differences in commonly observed instructor traits, such as rank, faculty status, and salary, have virtually no effect on student outcomes. . . . What does matter is instructors' perceived effectiveness and related subjective measures of quality evaluated by students."

The professors report other benefits beyond just learning more. "Students with instructors that tend to receive high evaluations are less likely to [drop] a course, more likely to receive better grades, and somewhat more likely to take similar courses in following years."

This study may seem to suggest that students should simply pick instructors with the highest ratings. Not so fast! A second study, published in 2010 by Professors Carrell and West, used a similar methodology but with two twists. First, in a design similar to a medical clinical trial, students were randomly assigned to the different instructors. Second, this report examined both the short- and long-term impact of professors' attributes.

Summarizing their findings, Professors Carrell and West wrote, "We find that less experienced and less qualified professors produce students who perform significantly better in the contemporaneous course being taught, whereas more experienced and highly qualified professors produce students who perform better in the follow-on related curriculum." In short, to understand instructor effectiveness, it is important to look both at the short and long term.

Finally, the value of evaluations depends not just on the instructor, but also on the student. Consider Valentine who was touring a high school that she was considering. Her student tour guide loved the school, but said, "Look out for eleventh-grade history class—the teacher is a nightmare. I am getting a D."

Several years later, Valentine remembers the 'nightmare' teacher as one of her favorites. The teacher had high expectations and demanding requirements, yet created rich learning opportunities. Such a teacher can be a nightmare for some students but perfect for others, such as conscientious Valentine.

What is the bottom line? Student evaluations of instructors are easily available and provide useful information. Picking the best instructor for an individual, however, requires far more than simply selecting highly rated instructors.

Let's take a look at a few instructor evaluations of the types you might encounter. Try to identify the specific bits of information in these actual student reviews that could hold particular value for you.

Kevin—who went on to become a best-selling author—wrote this about one of his English professors at Colorado University:

> *Professor M was completely open to anything. He came to class convinced that he had as much to learn from his students as we did from him. He also knew a thing or two about writing from his beautiful translations of other writers. I loved that during the first minutes of the first class it was clear that he knew so much more about writers, fiction, and writing than anyone I had ever known, and yet he had no ego.*

Or:

Kaycee—who ended up attending graduate school in psychology—wrote this this about her Intro Psych instructor:

Remarkable! Hard, but with fair tests. I felt like I should switch my major so I could take more classes with her. . . . Loved, loved, loved this class. Truly life-changing! . . . Provocative, challenging, and just plain awesome! . . . Maybe the warmest, most engaging person I have ever met.

Negative comments, too, can provide useful information (and sometimes can be entertaining) as students try to capture the essence of their instructors' inadequacies and demotivating styles.

You can't cheat in her class because no one knows the answers. Bring a pillow to the class so when you lose consciousness your head won't slam on your desk. And bring a pillow for your pillow, because your pillow will fall asleep too.

Peel away the layers of his superadded bombast and you get very little, maybe a whimpering thought, a distant muffled howl, a cry for help.

She is miserable and misery loves company. Annoying and speaks like her mouth is full of marbles. . . . She is an awful teacher.

Exploring instructor reviews, it is clear that some students end up in the wrong class for them. How does this happen? Some may simply be unaware that a better option for them is available. Others, however, may have made a trade-off. "I know Prof. B would be better for me, but I can have my Fridays free for my work-study job if I choose Prof. A." Or, "I can graduate a full term earlier if I bite the bullet and take the snoozer instructor's class this semester."

Our advice here is two-fold. First, if you are going to make a trade-off and choose the worse instructor for you, understand what you are choosing and why. Second, be willing to "pay" more to find great instructors. Compromise in other areas—such as your desire for a convenient schedule—in order to take the instructors who will be best for you.

This second bit of advice, we realize, may not be particularly compelling. In most areas of life, people already know what they *ought* to do. Yet they often still choose the other path. It is practically a rite of passage: boring adults must give trite advice to younger people, who will ignore it.

Neither a borrower nor a lender be, For loan oft loses both itself and friend, And borrowing dulls the edge of husbandry.

In modern language:

Do not borrow or loan money. If you loan money to a friend, you are likely to lose the money and your friend. Borrowing leads to wasting money.

Seems like reasonable advice? Yes. These lines from *Hamlet*, however, are actually intended as trite advice given by a father (Polonius) to a son (Laertes) who will not heed the advice.

Telling you to get up early to take a great instructor or to let a fantastic class interfere with a fun social event is exactly the boring old 'Polonius' advice that people tend to ignore. We can't stop ourselves from providing this advice, however. It's that important. In the words of a student reviewer: "I waited a semester to take this class with Instructor A and it was one hundred percent worth it."

Steven Covey made over $100 million with his book *Seven Habits of Highly Effective People*. First on his list of habits is "Be Proactive."

When it comes to selecting instructors, we implore you to be proactive. The alternative approach is to shuffle off to class with whichever instructors happen to fit in your schedule. Then spend your term complaining about miserable lectures, pointless problem sets, and being disappointed by the lack of inspiring and engaging courses. If this is your path, take the advice given earlier to buy a pillow for your pillow. It will fall asleep, too.

Rather than a pair of pillows, however, we suggest that you invest the time and effort to choose a) teachers with great styles and methods that b) can best provide you with what *you* need.

Take Home Messages

1. Each student has considerable power to select their instructors. Picking the good instructors and avoiding the bad ones is central to college success.

2. College instruction is hugely variable in quality. Two instructors in adjacent classrooms, teaching the same course, may be as different as night and day.

3. Decades of research evidence is clear: teacher quality is at (or near) the top of the list of the most important factors influencing student learning and career success.

4. There are multiple dimensions of teaching; comparing teachers on one summary measure is not wise. Consequently, there is no single metric for identifying a "best teacher."

OFFICE HOURS

How to Get the Most from Your Instructors When You Control the Agenda

Do you *really* need a lesson about office hours? After all, your parents and school counselors and just about everyone else have hammered home the message. Well, although it probably will come as a surprise, it is quite likely that you do need such a lesson.

For starters, most of the tips you will find about office hours are uninspired and vague: "You really ought to go." "It's an important opportunity to get to know your instructors." "Make sure to bring questions about material that has confused you."

Worse still, much of the advice is wrong. If you search for "office hours college advice," you are likely to find something like this, "The number one reason to go to office hours is to learn the material from class." This advice is simply not true.

In this chapter, we present both a strategy for office hours, and specific tactics. The strategy is grounded in an under-appreciated secret about office hours, a secret that is critically important in helping you to gain a deep, true, and useful education from college. The tactics include an arsenal of specific questions that you can modify to suit your own experience and needs, and use immediately.

The Secret

When it comes to office hours, unlike lectures and most other components of your courses, the agenda is determined and controlled by **you**. This is the key to getting the most out of office hours. You are free to dictate the agenda. And the most valuable item that you can put on your office hours agenda is rarely additional "content delivery."

Don't misunderstand this point. Hearing your instructor give additional descriptions of ideas and examples from class is absolutely helpful. But that's not the issue. The issue is that there are *better* uses of office hours. This is because numerous effective avenues of content delivery already exist. There are lectures, discussion sections, your textbooks, study guides, online learning tools, teaching assistants, and fellow students.

Office hours present a unique opportunity to explore deeper issues that transcend the course content. These include strategies for learning, the development of research motivations, the nature of intellectual passions, the poorly mapped road from college to the outside world, and much more.

To arrive at their current position, your instructors each have forged a long and personal path of intellectual development. Along that path they have learned deep, and not always obvious, truths about learning and education. To get the most out of your own college experience, you'll want to discover many of those same truths.

———————————

By tapping into your instructors' experiences and knowledge, you can benefit from the wisdom they have acquired, rather than stumbling around on your own. Identifying and acquiring this "wisdom" sounds a bit abstract and esoteric. It doesn't have to be.

One of the core principles of this book is that you, the student, will have better outcomes if you consider the world from the perspective of the instructor. Get outside of your head and into theirs.

When it comes to office hours, what is the instructor expecting and what sort of interaction will be productive for both sides? Recall that most instructors chose their current job over other positions that pay more, precisely because they want to have meaningful interactions with students, and help students learn and grow.

What do you the student want from office hours? At the transactional extreme, you may want some one-on-one tutoring on the content to improve your next exam score. Now, take a moment to think about this from the instructor's view. Does the instructor want to be treated simply as a tool to your next score? Probably not. The instructor is likely to find the experience more satisfying if there is a richer, deeper discussion, perhaps even including non-content-related discussion.

What have you enjoyed about the course? What aspects of the instructors' approach to teaching have you found helpful? To the extent that the office hours visit touches on these issues, the instructor may be more interested and engaged. After all, instructors may know very little about your life and your experiences in school and in the course. That information can be interesting and enhance their ability to give you value.

Before strategizing about what you'll say once you get to office hours, you may have to overcome your fear of putting yourself in that situation. Office hours can be intimidating. In fact, this is one of the chief reasons why more than half of students report that they rarely or never attend. (Author admission: This is why Jay did not attend office hours a single time during his undergraduate years.)

Concerns about embarrassing yourself, or sounding childish, or appearing incompetent—some of the very real manifestations of imposter syndrome—are often responsible for students not attending office hours, too. These fears can be powerful and seriously demotivating.

Taking steps to address and overcome these issues can be useful. One strategy can be to carefully prepare. You don't need a full script, with all your lines carefully planned. Erring on the over-prepared side, however, can go a long way to reducing your anxiety and giving you the necessary confidence.

To get you started, here are specific questions that may help you. As you read them, ask yourself if you know how your professors will respond and whether it would be useful to know how they'd respond.

On being a better student
- If you were a student in this class, how would you spend your study time? How does this differ from how you actually spent your time when you were a student?
- What surprises you most about student behavior?
- If you could change students in one way, what would it be?
- What do you consider the least efficient way to spend your study time?

On teaching and learning
- What is your process for writing exams? How do you decide what to include or not include?

- What do you think are the elements of an ideal exam question? Why?
- To what extent do you think instructors have a responsibility for finding and highlighting the *relevance* of material to students' lives?
- What is your process for creating a lecture? How do you begin?
- Do you have a process for improving your lectures and courses?
- Does technology enhance or constrain your teaching in any important ways?
- Students vary tremendously in many ways including work habits and prior training. Do you target one particular segment within a class? Why? And how?
- Do you have a "philosophy of teaching"? How has it changed over the years?

On choosing a major

- If you did college over, what would you do differently when selecting your classes?
- What mistakes do you think students make in selecting a major?

On learning about academic disciplines

- What are two or three of the biggest misconceptions that students have about your discipline? Where do these fallacies originate?
- If you were starting graduate study today, what topics would most interest you?
- What have been your biggest struggles and missteps in conducting research?

On learning what makes your instructor tick

- What is your least favorite part of your job? How has that changed over the years?

- Which fields do you think are the most intellectually rich today? Which are on the wane?
- Do you have any heroes in your field?

On understanding how an expert views the material of your course

- What are your biggest peeves about the textbooks we use?
- Are there intellectual topics in our course that you are unusually enthusiastic about? Why?

What is the purpose in asking these questions? 1) They'll help you perform better in that instructor's class. 2) They'll teach you important lessons that aren't covered explicitly in any class, but that are necessary for your overall success in college. And 3) because your instructors are uniquely positioned to answer these questions, you can't access this knowledge anywhere else.

You'll also be engaging your instructor in an unexpected and interesting way. Typically, this will set you apart from other students and help you begin building rapport.

———————————

At the opposite end of the spectrum, some office hours strategies will guarantee that you make a poor impression on your instructor.

Do Nothing beyond Asking for Answers

Isabella, a student in a finance class, came to Terry's office hours. She shuffled in with her heavy backpack and sat down, pulled out her copy of the weekly problem set, and began talking immediately:

> **Isabella:** Can you go over problem 1? Also, I have questions about other problems.

> **Terry:** Have you looked at the posted answers with the associated spreadsheet?
>
> **Isabella:** No.

How many less-than-ideal choices did Isabella make?

1: She did not ask Terry if it was a good time for them to speak.
2: She did not introduce herself or give any context for her visit, e.g., "Hi. I'm Isabella, from Finance at 11am on Mondays."
3: She jumped right into details. Although you do not want to idly waste time, a brief setup is always warranted. "I am enjoying the class. I have a few questions regarding Problem Set #7. Would you mind if I ask you about it?"
4: Prior to office hours, she neglected to examine the solutions that Terry had carefully written and made available.

Ask for a Personalized Lecture

Manav entered Terry's office and began:

> **Manav:** Hey Professor. I missed lecture yesterday. Could you quickly go over what you discussed?
>
> **Terry:** Have you looked at the notes with someone from class?
>
> **Manav:** Not yet. But just give me the big points.

As with Isabella, Manav could have improved this interaction. He did not knock or introduce himself and he asked to be spoon-fed information. Furthermore, Manav did all of this without having made any effort himself, and without following the path laid out by the instructor. Manav's approach shows little respect for the instructor's time.

Troll for Exam Questions

When Terry was a student, he had a famous economist as a professor. Fifteen years later, Terry had the famous instructor's son, Pierre, as his student. The student arranged an office hour visit ahead of time, along with dropping off his resume before the meeting.

Pierre's approach reflected his understanding of an instructor's world: he arranged a time in advance and included some background information. At the arranged time, he arrived, knocked, and re-introduced himself. All of this was *very* well done.

At that point, however, Pierre simply asked vague questions about the course material and the upcoming exam. He offered no thoughts about the course or its relevance for him. Nor did he clarify his reasons for wanting to meet. Rather, he made indirect probes regarding the exam, to which Terry repeated what he had said in class.

Terry's interpretation of the meeting was that Pierre was trolling for hints about what would be on the exam. Presumably some instructors reveal exam content during such visits, and Pierre may have used this to his advantage over the years.

———————

So you're prepared to attend office hours, you're aware of some less-than-effective strategies, and are confident that you can avoid those pitfalls. How can you get things started?

Breaking the Ice

Beyond the stress of simply attending office hours, it can be particularly intimidating to speak up and ask non-traditional, broad, philosophical, and personal questions such as these. This is especially challenging if your instructors' office hours consist of all attendees sitting together in the office.

At best, your fellow students may be caught off-guard or taken aback by the unexpected direction of your questions. At worst, they'll give you the evil eye and a heavy sigh to convey annoyance that you are reducing the rate of content delivery that they want.

Most students, it turns out, mistakenly assume that office hours is strictly an occasion for content delivery. But don't be bullied into allowing them to control the agenda; office hours is not their own personal tutoring session. It is helpful to take a few minutes ahead of time to consider your opening.

With the proper phrasing, you can introduce your change-of-direction in a way that highlights: 1) that it's a serious line of discussion; 2) that it has relevance for your class and for your education; and 3) that your instructor is exactly the right person with the expertise to respond. Here are a few starters:

- I think I have a good understanding of the material that you've presented in class. Would you mind if I ask a "bigger picture" question?
- I'm really enjoying this class and want to learn more about this field. Would it be okay if I ask you some questions that are more about the discipline in general?
- Although I did well in high school, I've struggled since coming to college. You've spent a lot of time in the college environment and have experience with many students. May we talk a bit about the mechanics of studying and learning, and how I might improve in these areas?

There is always time for a brief introduction. In *Pulp Fiction*, Harvey Keitel plays the "problem-solver," Winston Wolf. When "The Wolf" arrives, several characters are under impossibly intense time pressure. Unexpectedly, he very calmly introduces himself. It seems to take an eternity in such a pressure-packed moment, yet the introduction takes a mere eleven seconds. Importantly, it sets a tone of respect, professionalism, and efficiency.

When you attend office hours think of The Wolf. Take eleven seconds to make a positive impression.

- "My name is Pedram. I am interested in conservation and environmental studies. I took Ecology from you last quarter and couldn't stop telling my roommates all the cool things you taught us in class. Would you mind if I ask you a question about population bottlenecks?"
- "My name is Soo-Yee, but I go by Becky. I am an exchange student from South Korea. I've loved your stories in class about working at Goldman, Sachs & Co. I was hoping to learn a bit more about the background of options pricing; I can do the math, but I am struggling with the intuition. Can you help me understand why "put" prices sometimes increase when there is good news on a stock? That is the exact opposite of what I would expect."

It's even okay if your brief introduction simply lets the instructor understand that you're new to office hours and are confused. "My name is Annika and I've never been to office hours. I'm feeling nervous and not even sure exactly what I'm looking for. But I am enjoying your class and excited about what we're learning."

The Protocol

One small but important reminder: regardless of the specific details of your office hours interactions, certain protocol is essential.

Be polite.
- Knock. Don't just walk in.
- Ask your instructor if they are available (even if you are visiting during stated office hours).
- When leaving, thank the instructor for their time and for their efforts in the class.

Be considerate.

- Even after repeated visits, continue to introduce yourself, quickly stating your name and the class you are in. Do this before the instructor is able to say that she knows that already.
- Don't assume that the instructor remembers the details of your previous interactions.

Be respectful.

- Do not stay longer than the posted office hours.
- Don't show up unannounced at non-office hours times.

Be prepared.

- If the office hours is a small group, rather than individual meetings, it's okay if you don't have any questions. But let the instructor know this: "I don't have any specific questions today; I'd just like to listen in, if that's okay."
- If you have an agenda, be prepared to articulate it clearly and concisely.
- View the interaction as a give and take, not just a take. Give thoughtful responses to your instructor's questions.

Take Home Messages

1. Office hours allows the student to control the agenda. Consider office hours as a unique opportunity to gain insight into the world from a person with a long history within education and a perspective that is likely very different from yours or from those people around you.

2. Engage your instructor in novel ways. In doing so, you have the opportunity to create a different and better relationship with someone who has spent their life in the academy. Your instructor has much to offer and can become a mentor.

3. Avoid common office hours pitfalls: the hurried point grab, the time-wasting empty visit, and the obvious exam-question trolling. These behaviors send a clear message that you believe your grade is more important than your relationship with the course, the content, and the instructor.

4. Be mindful of protocol. Introduce yourself. Be polite, brief, and interesting. Be well prepared.

CLASSROOM BEHAVIOR

How to Master Content and Make a Positive Impression on Your Instructor

Miranda, a former student of Terry's, popped her head into his office one day and said, "I have wonderful news." She entered, sat down, and began her explanation. After extensive research, many interviews, and reading about a variety of jobs and careers, Miranda had come to a big decision. "I've found the perfect job for me; I want to be an economic consultant. It's a small niche in the big world, but it lines up with my interests and plans perfectly."

Then Miranda asked, "Can you help me get a job?" To this, Terry replied, "I wish that I could, but there's nothing I can do to help you with this. I'm really sorry." Miranda left, never to be heard from again (by Terry).

Unbeknownst to Miranda, Terry had previously worked for one of the leading economic consulting firms in the world. Furthermore, one of the senior partners of that firm had literally said to Terry, "I will hire anyone you recommend, sight unseen."

Here's a bit of additional information: Miranda was super smart with a math degree from an Ivy League school. She also had one of the top scores in Terry's graduate economics course. Finally, you should know that Terry has worked hard and gone to extreme lengths to get many students amazing jobs.

Why did Terry not help Miranda? Read the following stories first. Then we will return to Miranda's situation.

Bianca was an undergraduate student of Jay's at UCLA, during her first year. She earned a B+ in his course. Later, when Bianca applied to medical school, Jay wrote a detailed and persuasive letter of recommendation on her behalf, which played a pivotal role in her acceptance to medical school.

All recommendation letters from professors start with the same information. How do you know the applicant and, if it was through a class, what grade did the student earn? Jay's letter included this information:

> Dear Admissions Committee,
>
> It is a pleasure to write this letter in support of Bianca P for admission to your medical school. During her first year at UCLA, I served as her professor for Life Sciences 2: *Cells, Tissues, and Organs.* She earned a B+, putting her in the top half of all the students taking the course.

This inauspicious beginning seems unlikely to help any student achieve anything at all. However, this formulaic and mediocre start was followed by:

> **[MAGIC WORDS that changed Bianca's life.]**

What were those magic words? Well, the specific words actually aren't the most important thing here, because they're not the same for everyone. Also, without context, their value isn't always immediately apparent. So, here's a bit of the Bianca backstory.

Bianca always sat in the second row of the large classroom. Bianca arrived five minutes early for every class, took notes on paper, never used her cell phone or laptop, was engrossed in the lectures, and conveyed interest with her eye contact and body language. She concentrated during the hard parts. She showed the appropriate response—surprise, laughter, disbelief—to the photographs and other content presented.

Sometimes as Bianca was leaving, she would make a quick comment to Jay: "Great lecture, Professor. That story about the FBI crime lab was really cool."

Bianca also came to office hours several times. When she did, she had genuine and thoughtful questions that conveyed reflection and engagement. For example, "I am loving what you've been teaching us about the evolution of altruistic behavior! That was really interesting to learn why female squirrels were more altruistic than males. I'm leaning toward becoming a psychology major and would love to learn more about the research people are doing on this topic. Do you have any suggestions for additional reading?"

After such a question, Bianca would always follow up. Sometimes in person, but often just in a note. "I just wanted to thank you. In answer to my question about the evolution of alarm calls, you suggested the Paul Sherman paper. I tracked the paper down, and enjoyed learning how the scientists conducted the research on the evolution of such behavior."

So, *how did Jay help Bianca get into medical school?* What were the magic words he wrote? In part, this is what he said:

> Once in a great while a person comes along, so bursting with intelligence, charisma, energy, and potential that I actually look forward to an opportunity to write on his or her behalf. Bianca P is such a person . . .

In the three years since meeting her, I have had dozens of substantive interactions with Bianca as she has explored her academic interests, developed those interests, and identified meaningful potential career paths. During these meetings I have seen her transition from a confused student struggling to acquire the necessary study skills into the poised and competent person she is. Throughout this maturation, Bianca's desire to learn has been a constant. She relates issues in her courses to ideas she encounters in literature, psychology, math, and current events. She sees relationships and connections that most students do not. And, importantly, during our interactions, Bianca has come to exhibit an exceptional sense of maturity and responsibility . . .

Bianca P is unquestionably motivated, has an exceptional and nuanced grasp of biology, and possesses the intellectual potential to become successful in the field of medicine. She has shared with me an unusually large number of original ideas and engaged me in remarkably stimulating and challenging conversations . . .

Jay couldn't change the fact that Bianca got a B+ in his class. He could, however, highlight those many features of Bianca that are critically important to admissions committees but aren't apparent from an applicant's transcripts and test scores. Those factors can be just the nudge that tips a committee's decision from neutral to positive.

Just prior to a class for 400 students, Jay was writing an outline on the board. A student walked in and, before sitting down, came up to him and said, "I have a quick question about my exam." Holding their exam up, they continued, "In my answer, I have everything from the posted answer key, but I didn't get all of the points." Jay responded, "Hi. Can we please talk after lecture?"

If you could hear inside Jay's brain at the moment before class begins, the noise would be deafening.

Are my eleven teaching assistants here in the correct part of the auditorium and are they distributing the handouts? Is my opening photo of the lizard running across water queued up correctly to align with the polar bond slide that I will show on the second screen?

Is the battery in my wireless microphone fully charged? Is the music that I am playing on the correct track and at a good volume? How do I pace the punchline of the joke that leads into the water surface-tension section to create maximum humor and teaching effect? Is my shirt tucked in? Is there any food in my teeth?

For many instructors, particularly with large classes, one of their most important teaching-related desires is this: *Please do not speak to me in the few minutes before a lecture.*

If you find yourself tempted to break this rule, first ask yourself: How would you feel if you were about to speak to 400 people? Would you have a lot on your mind and a strong need to focus your thoughts? A lecture may look easy, but, as with any performance, it is complicated. To perform well, the instructor needs significant mental preparation, particularly in the last few minutes before class begins. Prior to lecture, an instructor is in a similar physiological state as a boxer moments before the start of round one.

Put more broadly: students should be conscious of their professors as human beings. Therefore, students will do better if they approach their professors at opportune times for the professor, and, in many cases, this will be after instead of before class.

———————

When Terry was in graduate school he audited, without being formally enrolled to earn a grade, a course taught by Professor Marty Feldstein. An accomplished economist, Professor Feldstein's credits include having been the chairman of the Council of Economic Advisors to President Reagan. At Harvard, Professor Feldstein taught the single most popular college course at the school.

Terry was so impressed with the college course that he decided to attend Professor Feldstein's macroeconomic graduate course. Terry had already completed the coursework required for his degree, so he was taking the class purely for education. No grade, no credits. Just knowledge.

One day, Professor Feldstein was reviewing background information on finance that students would need for an upcoming exam. Because Terry already understood that material, he was bored and began reading a physical newspaper. The class only had about twelve students and after a few minutes (and some page turning by Terry), Professor Feldstein had a mini explosion, "Terry, if you are going to read the newspaper, I'd prefer that you leave."

To this day, Terry is mortified by his behavior. Reading the newspaper in a twelve-person class with one of the world's most famous economists? How could anyone be so rude? The answer is that for many of us, these basic rules of respect become obvious only after the fact. (Note to readers: It is *painfully* embarrassing to recount a story like this. We're only enduring that feeling in the hopes that we can spare you the same.)

Jay is always looking for inspiring and unexpected photos to show in class to complement his lectures. In a lecture on gift-giving and its relationship to the biological basis for altruism, he showed photos of people receiving "Swiftmas" presents. Swiftmas is a term used to describe singer Taylor Swift's surprise gift-giving. Importantly, Jay did not discuss the photo; he simply displayed images while talking about the joy created by surprise gifts.

After the lecture, however, a student wrote Jay a fun, smart note. The note was specific in praising both the idea—gift-giving and its relevance to the biological theories they had been discussing in class for the past week—and the implementation.

"You picked the perfect image that captures Taylor Swift's genius. I love that you did that." Reading the note, Jay was entertained and grateful for the validation of his efforts in finding provocative photos. The effect of the note was that the student made a huge, positive impression on Jay. If and when the opportunity arises, Jay will be strongly inclined to help this student.

———————

Let's return to poor Miranda, from the beginning of this chapter, who could have had her dreams fulfilled if she had understood and followed the unwritten rules. To recap, Miranda was an extremely smart student who desired a job in an industry in which Terry had great connections. Why did Terry not help Miranda?

The answer is that at least half a dozen times during the semester Miranda had made Terry's life worse. These included disrespectful comments in class, requests for special treatment, complaints about her grade, and regular disruptions of the class by arriving late and talking. Even when she came to Terry's office seeking help, she sat right down without asking if he had time to talk.

Imagine that Terry had arranged for Miranda to get a job. How would she have performed in that job? She was unquestionably smart. But Terry feared (and suspected) that, based on her previous behavior, she would most likely make her boss's life worse, rather than better. Recommending such a person would hurt the employer and harm Terry's relationship with the firm, leading to poorer job opportunities in the future for other students.

To make this point concrete, in the next chapter we meet Faizah, a student of Terry's, who with his recommendation became one of the first Chapman University students to work for Goldman, Sachs & Co. Because she did such a fantastic job, Faizah validated Terry's recommendation; this has led to dozens more Chapman students working at Goldman.

Take Home Messages

1. Students can make a strong impression on an instructor, even in a huge lecture. Behave in a manner that will help the instructor write a great letter on your behalf in the future. It's more valuable for a recommendation to say that the instructor has seen a student change and improve than that they've just always been smart.

2. Instructors are people, too. They remember the actions of students. You are not invisible. Even in a large class, your behavior is likely to be memorable to the instructor, particularly if it is funny, courteous, or rude. You must actively work to enhance and protect your reputation at all times.

3. Refrain from asking your instructor any questions in the minutes just before class. Wait until after class or send a nice note that the instructor can answer at their leisure, when they can give their response the thought it deserves.

4. When you like a lecture, tell your instructor! Make the compliment specific to accentuate its credibility. Convey it in a way that requires no response from the instructor.

5. Good instructors look forward to being able to help their students. In order to do this effectively, we are evaluating students on much more than their scores and grades.

NURTURING YOUR RELATIONSHIPS WITH INSTRUCTORS

The Path to Recommendations, a Mentor, Jobs, and More

Four years after graduating from college, twenty-five-year-old Faizah navigated her way through a crowded New York City subway platform to an interview for her dream job at a leading financial firm. Excited and nervous, Faizah was reassured by two notes she had received earlier in the day from her former instructor, Terry, assuring her that she would be well received and had an excellent chance of landing a job.

In fact, Terry had paved the way by introducing Faizah to the owner of the firm, and by providing specific advice. What did Faizah do to warrant this guidance from her former instructor, and a private entrée to the one job in the world she had singled out as best for herself?

Over the course of many years, Faizah had developed and nurtured a mentorship with Terry. Developing an effective mentorship with an instructor can look easy, natural, and spontaneous; in some cases, it actually is. But it's far too important to your success in college and life to approach haphazardly, simply *hoping* that you get the best outcomes.

Having healthy and substantive professional relationships with instructors will enrich your education and provide knowledge and wisdom far beyond the curriculum. It will open doors to jobs, graduate school admissions, scholarships, and more. For these reasons, you need to plan these relationships and guide their growth.

Reggie Gilyard spent some years as the dean of the Chapman Business School. At his going away lunch he was asked, "What would you like as your legacy?" To this, Dean Gilyard replied, "I got the students jobs." Just as Reggie Gilyard focused on helping students, many professors devote, and pride themselves, on their mentorship of many successful students.

Students want mentors, and instructors want to be mentors. Shouldn't this be easy? Perhaps. But all relationships between people are complicated. Anyone with a parent, sibling, friend, or romantic partner knows this all too well. It certainly helps that both students and instructors can provide something that the other side wants. But there's more to it; finding a good mentor requires strategy, tactics, effort, and luck.

Developing professional relationships is a skill that falls between the cracks of traditional course offerings. It's psychology. But it's also negotiation. And art. And writing. And manners. And animal behavior. And debate. And public speaking. And conversation. There are many good ways to build these relationships, but we think it's helpful to view the process as having five phases:

1. Have a relationship strategy. Seek out professional relationships with instructors you like, and who work in areas that interest you.
2. Make initial contact in an honest, thoughtful manner.
3. Find opportunities to deepen your relationships.
4. Stay in contact without creating a burden.

5. Identify specific payoffs: mentorships, recommendation letters, jobs.

Let's explore them.

1. Have a Relationship Strategy

Brandee was finishing an economics PhD program at Harvard. One day, as she walked to campus, she happened to see Professor Singh, the person in charge of hiring economists that year for the Harvard Kennedy School faculty.

Brandee stopped and said, "Hello, I'm sorry to bother you, but I was wondering about my job application." Professor Singh replied that he would check, and a few minutes later called with the bad news that Brandee had not made it past the first step; she would not be invited for an interview.

This news was like a stomach punch. When Brandee got to her office, she went to see her graduate school advisor, Professor Elinor, with whom she had a great relationship. On hearing the news that Brandee would not receive an interview, her mentor Elinor replied, "That's not right. Let me make a few calls."

Thirty minutes later, Professor Singh called Brandee again. He did not mention the previous rejection or their earlier encounter, and said, "We are pleased to offer you an interview." Professor Elinor helped Brandee get many such opportunities. (Elinor subsequently won a Nobel Prize in economics, and Brandee is a tenured professor at a top school.)

Although Brandee's grades in graduate school were excellent, they were far from being the best in her class. She had, however, developed a strong bond with Professor Elinor, primarily by helping with Elinor's research. Brandee furthered her own career by first helping her advisor achieve her goals. Such is the nature of productive relationships.

The value of strong professional relationships with your instructors can be extreme. People like Faizah and Brandee have guardian angels that help them at each stage. Phone calls are made, doors are magically opened, and success seems effortless.

Many students, however, pass through college like a car on a factory assembly line. Each year, each class is an unremarkable step in a march toward graduation. This assembly line approach works for some people. They may even find success. Nevertheless, we urge students to increase their chances of a future with great options.

The benefits to having strong, positive professional relationships with your instructors include learning more, having more fun, and being more successful. Benefits also include concrete dividends, such as compelling letters of recommendation and assistance getting jobs.

Let's move toward a more specific plan of action. A college student has ten or more instructors per year, for a total of 20–50 instructors over the course of a two- or four-year program. It's not practical to have meaningful beyond-the-classroom relationships with dozens of instructors. So each student needs a strategy for cultivating and nurturing relationships.

In sales, there is a 10-3-1 rule of thumb. Ten meetings lead to three good prospects which lead to one sale. Similarly, with relationships it is possible to engineer introductions with your ten instructors in a year, leading to multiple contacts with about three. And from these, perhaps one relationship extends beyond the end of college.

2. Make Initial Contact in an Honest, Thoughtful Manner

We suggest that you create a positive, initial contact with each instructor, each term. This can be as simple as a three-line note or a five-minute visit to office hours (see chapter 7, on office hours, for more details). The total effort needed to create a positive first contact can be less than one hour per year. This is a trivial investment of time. But it can generate enormous benefits. Look at how easy this can be.

Laying the Groundwork

> Subject: best LS4 lecture ever
>
> Dr. Phelan,
>
> I felt compelled to write you. Today was the best LS4 lecture I have attended all quarter. The chicken co-dominance study, the evolution of antibiotic resistance, a young T.H. Morgan, and the raccoon pic were just a few highlights. I was positively giddy during and after lecture. I eagerly await your next lecture on Friday.
>
> Sincerely, Julissa A
>
> ps—I really enjoyed the group lunch I had with you back in the day when I was enrolled in LS2 Spring quarter 2018. You gave me life advice that really came through for me. Thanks!

This is a great first note. It is positive. It contains specific, fun references that reveal it is genuine. It connects back to previous interactions. It makes no demands. Any instructor would be thrilled to receive this note, and yet almost no students send these communications. When Julissa needs something in the future, this initial note will increase her chances enormously.

In the appendix to this chapter we have included numerous other real notes from students. For each, we provide comments and critiques.

Q: Can you fake it?

Here is a revealing exercise. Write a praising note like Julissa's to an instructor you did not like. Think of the most boring, mean, disorganized, inarticulate instructor you have had.

For most people, such a disingenuous letter is almost impossible to write. We can learn two lessons from this task. First, make contact very early in the relationship, before you have solidified a firm impression. Even if the first lecture is weak, you can find something positive to say. "Peeking ahead on the syllabus, I am looking forward to learning about plants in chapter 8. I had a Venus fly trap when I was in 2nd grade."

Second, always tell the truth. You cannot build a good relationship on a foundation of lies. Find something positive that is true, and deliver that message.

Crafting a Pitch That Works

Suppose you would like to gain research experience. This is a good idea for many reasons, but we're not going to discuss those right now. Rather, we're going to use this question for learning how to interact effectively with your professors.

We'll explore this primarily by evaluating some actual student attempts. Most were effective, but some were spectacularly ineffective. In developing your own pitch, incorporate information that will increase your odds of success.

- What value do you have? What sets you apart?
- How will you make the instructor's life easier/better?

- Have you done your homework? How have you demonstrated this?
- Do you communicate clearly and concisely?

Making the Pitch—Nolan's Blunder

Date: Wed, 22 Feb
Subject: Research

Hey Professor, I am looking for a research position and I want to know if you do research and need any students.

Best, Nolan

Q: Will this get a good response? How would you improve it?
This note from Nolan is probably worse than none. Nolan conveys no enthusiasm. He includes no motivation for why he wants to work on a particular project. For all we know, this exact note could have been sent to thousands of professors around the world. If so, it would have been unsuccessful globally.

As with the introductory notes, in the appendix of this chapter we include slightly redacted versions of other notes from students looking for research experience. Again, we provide comments and critiques.

3. Find Opportunities to Deepen Your Relationships

Bob was a young military officer sent to deliver documents to the White House one evening many years ago. While waiting for a signature, he encountered Mark, an older man with a serious demeanor. Bob struck up a conversation with Mark, pushing through the awkwardness of what felt like a mostly one-sided conversation.

In the years after their chance meeting, Bob did everything he could to keep in touch with Mark. Should Bob go to law school or was it not worth the time? Should Bob quit law school and take a job as a newspaper writer at *The Washington Post*?

Bob described his years-long strategy for developing a relationship with Mark (and others).

> *I expended a great deal of energy trying to find things or people who were interesting. . . . He [Mark] showed no interest in striking up a long conversation, but I was intent on it. . . . I kept in touch with [Mark] through phone calls to his office or home. We were becoming friends of a sort. He was the mentor . . . and I kept asking for advice. . . . Though I was busy in my new job, I kept Mark on my call list and checked in with him.*

What makes this relationship notable is that it led to the only resignation of a U.S. president. Bob is Bob Woodward of *The Washington Post*, and Mark is Mark Felt of the FBI. Together, the two took down President Nixon—Woodward working with Carl Bernstein as investigative reporters at *The Washington Post*, and Mark Felt secretly feeding information from the FBI under the cover name of "Deep Throat."

Bob Woodward has won nearly every major American journalism award and helped *The Washington Post* win the Pulitzer Prize twice. The relationships he cultivated were central to his success, and they did not occur by accident. Bob's relationship strategy was to identify important individuals and then cultivate relationships. This cultivation involved actions that were low cost to the other people. Who would refuse, for example, to give career advice to an appreciative and accomplished younger person?

You are unlikely to run into an FBI agent who will turn out to have evidence of crimes by the president. However, you are *very* likely to have opportunities to develop better relationships with your professors. Some of this may require guile and gumption. Some may be as simple as saying yes to an invitation.

Once, for example, Terry invited all of his seventy students to lunch with representatives from a high-profile finance firm. In the invitation Terry included these magic words, "By the way, this firm is hiring both summer interns and full-time employees. The work is very interesting, and the pay is high."

Anticipating a rush of applications for the employer-student lunch, Terry wrote, "There are limited slots for lunch. Six lucky students will be chosen randomly from all who apply before the deadline."

What happened? The lunch occurred. Two students at the lunch were asked to interview for jobs. And one was offered a job, accepted it, and still works at the firm. The only surprising aspect is this: out of seventy students, only three signed up for the lunch. There was no need for a lottery, and the job was ridiculously easy to obtain. So, if your instructor offers you free money in the form of introductions to employers, lunch opportunities, or anything else, say yes!

Other opportunities may be more subtle. In one class, for example, Terry asked for a volunteer to produce a resume book. Quick to volunteer was front-row Kaela. The total effort to collate the set of resumes was just an hour or two of Kaela's time. Now she has a great job in Stockholm working for one of Terry's best friends. Coincidence? Not at all. Kaela's willingness to help was memorable, and, in fact, Terry has not forgotten.

After meeting your instructors early in the term, prepare for your next steps. First, narrow down your full list to those people who inspire you and who might be able to help you. Second, find ways to interact with them further.

Here are some low-cost ways to facilitate having repeated interactions. Is the instructor holding any sort of event, such as a talk or an open house? If so, swing by and be a positive force. Does the instructor state that they need any help? This could be very minor. "I need these evaluations carried by a student to the office. Is anyone available?"

Look for opportunities with instructors who could be of "high value" to you. Perhaps your instructor has revealed an interest in something (even unrelated to the course)—"I'm a geography buff." "I'm obsessed with gardening." Or "I love movies." Or the professor incorporates beautiful photos/images in lecture presentations. These present opportunities for contact. "The images you've shown in class are so beautiful; I thought you might like the attached photo that I came across in *National Geographic*."

4. Stay in Contact without Creating a Burden

Four (or five) years is a long time. As your college experience plays out, you will have a variety of needs, many of which you cannot initially anticipate. It is wise to develop and maintain relationships with your professors, even when you have no immediate need for their help.

Playing the Long-Game

> Subject: Thank you
>
> Professor Phelan,
>
> I took your class as a mere general education requirement and am now inspired to pursue graduate work in biology. You have an

incredible gift for teaching and for somehow making a very large science class feel personal.

I greatly appreciated the time that you took after class to answer my odd questions about the mind, determinism, and biologists. I feel that knowing how the body works takes the "magic" out of life, yet I feel compelled to know more. My sense of awe once reserved for the mystical is now directed towards the intricate functions of the body and the brilliance of evolution.

Thank you for a truly life-changing quarter. Aside from forcing my family to read *Mean Genes*, I will definitely look to enroll in any Life Science classes you are teaching in the future.

Very Respectfully,

Arjun G

Q: How does this help? What does it help with?
A: This is a masterful note.

Context? Check.

Specific, relevant observations revealing that Arjun was paying deep attention? Check.

Praise? Check.

Provocative, thoughtful, personality-revealing comments? Check.

A touch of humor? Check.

A specific request? Actually: NO.

But make no mistake, when Arjun is looking for advice on graduate schools, guidance in the application process, or a recommendation letter, he has already laid the groundwork so that his professor will make every effort to help him get what he wants.

When are you done developing your relationships with your professors? In a word: never.

The key to a successful check-in is to view the interaction from the eyes of the instructor. First, if you ask a question, then the recipient has a burden to respond and the impact can switch from positive to negative. Second, stories are better than summaries. "Today my boss exclaimed, 'I loved your presentation. I suspect we'll be able to promote you soon.'" This is so much better than writing "work is going well." Finally, the note should be short—less than one or two minutes to read. In essence you are saying, "Hey Professor, I am doing well, in part because of what you taught me. Thanks."

5. Identify Specific Payoffs: Mentorships, Recommendation Letters, Jobs

Mentorships—The path to getting a mentor is not straightforward. Unfortunately, it's rarely effective to just ask someone to be your mentor. One useful strategy can be to seek help with a specific issue. Recall that Bob Woodward asked Mark Felt to weigh in on the choice between law school and writing for the *Washington Post*. This is fun and cool for the mentor.

Simply requesting additional instruction from the professor is less likely to lead to a mentor relationship. Assistance with broader challenges—provided that the instructor has given you reason to believe they are able and willing to help with them—

can open the door to a more mentor-like relationship. Consider Hans's approach.

A Mentor-Finding Strategy

Subject: LS2—Thanks

Professor,

I was up late last night, studying for today's final, when I realized how devastated I was that this class had come to an end. That may seem like a ridiculous statement, but my short UCLA career has seen me lose much of the drive that I brought with me. Getting caught in the Pre-Med trap unfortunately upset much of what I expected and wanted from college—I wanted to thank you for creating a classroom environment that reminded me of how awesome it can be to learn.

However, hindsight is 20/20, and, whether it was ego or embarrassment, I never sought you out in Office Hours or the like to relay that thanks.

That has left me with a question that I would like to ask: In one of our first classes this quarter, you spoke of your own academic difficulty as an undergraduate student at UCLA. What advice can you lend to an individual in much the same situation? What did you change about your habits as a student that allowed you to achieve what you have? I realize this is a vague question, probably best suited for someone who isn't so occupied (and rightly so) as yourself, but I wanted to ask, nonetheless.

Again, thank you for an amazing class—you have definitely opened my mind.

Best, Hans

Q: What makes this note good? What might come from it?

This is an excellent note, likely to receive a positive response. It's got all the hallmarks of a good note that we have already discussed: context, kindness and praise, interesting and engaging sentence construction. It also has a clear and specific request that seems appropriate. For this reason, it will likely lead to a response and a one-on-one meeting on a substantive matter. This is a very good way to initiate a relationship with the potential for future mentorship.

Recommendations—Writing recommendations on behalf of students requires significant effort and time from professors. But it's part of the job, so they understand and expect that they'll get requests. Nonetheless, take care when the time comes for this. With the proper approach, you can ensure that they provide the best possible recommendation for you.

Making the Recommendation Request

Subject: Letter of Recommendation

Hi Professor Phelan,

I hope that your year is going well. I'm not sure if you remember me, but my name is Alozie R. I was a student in your Life Science 2—Cell Biology and Physiology class during Winter 2016 and your Life Science 4—Genetics class during Summer 2016. I tried to make it to office hours whenever I could. With your help and the TAs' I was able to receive an A– in LS2 and an A in LS4.

Because I greatly respect you as an instructor, I would like to ask if you would be willing to write a favorable Letter of Recommendation for me as I am currently applying to medical school. I am asking you in particular because I really enjoyed your class. I appreciated how your lectures were always so lively and how the material of the class was represented through various ways, such as pictures on the screen or funny anecdotes that were related to the things we were learning in class.

You were definitely my favorite teacher at UCLA because of your small incorporations of entertainment with education, which is why I decided to take LS4 in the summer so that I could have you as my professor again. I strongly admire your dedication to the students that was seen by that one day during summer where you bought Diddy Reese cookies for everyone and how on the last day of lecture you gave a goodbye message of "Do good."

I'm truly sorry for not asking you about this request earlier when you may have known me better, and I realize that it might be difficult to remember specific things about me. However, I can send you my resume to help you get more acquainted with who I am. In addition, I can take the time to meet you whenever you are available, and you can get to know me on a more personal level, and I can answer any questions you may have. Hopefully, if you can indeed find it in your busy schedule, these can assist you in writing a Letter of Recommendation.

Once again, I understand that you have a busy schedule, but I would truly appreciate any reply. Thank you for your time.

Sincerely, Alozie R

Q: What is good with this request?

There is a consistent thread that runs through all of the effective letters we have included in this chapter, including Alozie's request for recommendation: context. Reminders of past interactions are extremely important—particularly if your professor has had hundreds of students.

Other features, too, can improve your outcomes: varied sentence structure, free from grammatical or word choice errors; an engaging style that allows your personality to shine through; specific details that set you apart, while reminding your professor of your particular style, personality, and future potential.

Q: Can you improve them?

When you request a recommendation, do everything you can to make your professor's job easier. Attach to the note (and deliver as a hardcopy) all of the necessary documents in a packet, making sure to give your professor sufficient time to write the letter (at least two weeks, but even more is better). These may include:

- your transcript
- a personal statement you have written about yourself
- all of the specific details about the position/schools to which you are applying
- a photo of yourself
- a clear statement of relevant deadlines

The personal statement is the portion that requires the most creativity and where you have the best chance to boost your odds of admission. After all, you cannot change your grades, but you can write a great essay. Applying the writing lessons of chapter 12, your personal statement for graduate school should align your goals with that of the school. Moreover, your writing should be concise, engaging, and even fun. Finally, be sure to leave time to revise.

And, of course, be sure to write a follow-up thank you note once the letter/recommendation has been received, and tell your instructor the outcome of your applications.

Take Home Messages

1. Have a relationship strategy. Over the course of your college career, seek to have positive relationships with multiple instructors and to develop at least one primary mentor.

2. Crafting a pitch that will get you a research position requires careful planning and surgical precision. Convey your value, your personality, and what sets you apart. Your instructor must have no doubts that you would make their life easier/better. Convey that you have done your homework. And communicate all of this clearly and concisely.

3. Seek to create a short, positive, and memorable interaction with each of your instructors early in the term. Identify those instructors who inspire you and who may be able to help you. Look for opportunities (easy or hard) to create contacts with the instructors in ways that are fun and low-effort for the instructor.

4. Don't neglect the long game. A kind, articulate, informative note without a request can pave the way for successful requests down the line. Keep in touch with the professors who have helped you. They'll appreciate feedback on how they have influenced their students. And they'll be happy to return the favor if and when you need additional help.

5. When the time comes to request a recommendation, give your professor the exact information they will need to write a personalized, effective recommendation that reflects your strengths and advances your needs.

Appendix: More Examples of Real Student Notes with Comments and Critiques

Laying the Groundwork

> Subject: Thank you
>
> Hi professor,
>
> I am a student from your LS–1 class this quarter. I am writing you this note because I regret not having said this in class directly to you. And it is probably easier for me to say this now than before because: 1. You don't know me. 2. I will no longer be seeing you and don't have to worry about whether I said this to kiss up, etc.
>
> Thank you very much for your teaching. You made the course material much more interesting to me. In addition to the course materials, the overall class atmosphere you created from your business attire to your careful lecture notes, problem sets on bright color papers, etc. etc. I don't know why it was so hard to say it in person—probably because I feared that you would interpret my intentions as trying to get on your good side, etc. which WOULD be true of certain professors. I mean with some of them you just don't feel that connection. And I'll stop because it seems like I'm kissing up more.
>
> Thank you. I enjoyed your course very much.
>
> Ronald

Q: What is good with this?

Ronald has done several things well here. First, he immediately gives context, explaining who he is and why he is writing. He also shows kindness, praising the instructor. Think about it. Do you ever tire of praise? Neither do professors. They are human. Importantly, Ronald is specific in his praise. That gives his note much more impact and value. It's clear that he has paid attention, even to the little details. Are you paying attention to the little details? It's never too late to begin or to improve.

Ronald does not ask for anything. Rather than making his letter useless, however, it increases the impact of subsequent interactions.

Q: How can you improve it?
Self-deprecation can be good—but does Ronald go too far? As an exercise, figure out how you could revise his note to improve it in this regard.

Making the Pitch—Madeline's Tome

> Subject: Research
>
> To Professor Phelan:
>
> On the first day of LS2, spring quarter 2016, I walked into LaKretz 110 with a vivid interest (and confidence) in biology. When I exited that classroom on Monday of finals week, I left with passion, motivation, (humility), and most importantly, the ability to methodically examine my surroundings. Each lecture provoked new thoughts and tested my perceptions of the world. Biology began to integrate itself in all my daily conversations: I would find myself expounding on the properties of caffeine to my friends. Yesterday, while I was helping my mother pronounce drug names, I was delighted that I understood that Wellbutrin acts like cocaine and that Xanax enhances GABA's inhibitory effects.
>
> After receiving a 65/100 on the second midterm, I wondered if, despite my interest, I was even capable of pursuing my dreams

in the sciences. However, this development merely unearthed my determination to fulfill my goals to the best of my ability. I don't think that I have ever worked harder for a class.

Professor Phelan, although you probably don't know who I am, you impacted my fundamental perceptions of the world and of myself. Therefore, I was wondering if you had any available positions in your lab, so that we could work together in the future. Your past research on caloric restriction and genetic influences greatly interests me. I believe that you will bring out the best in me and that I will work hard, with diligence and passion, to contribute to exciting discoveries in biology.

If you are interested, I have attached my curriculum vitae for your perusal and can provide references at your request. Regardless, thank you for your inspiration and dedication to the Life Science series. My only regret in taking this class with you was not attending more office hours.

Sincerely, Madeline Y

Q: What are the strengths of this letter?

Madeline has written an excellent letter and query about a research position. She gives context for who she is and why she is writing. She cites specific examples for why she has singled out this particular professor, with praise that is sincere. And her personality shines through.

Q: Can you improve it?

There still is room for improvement in Madeline's note. At more than 300 words, it is a bit longer than optimal. Also, she buries her request in the second sentence of the third paragraph. If her professor reads too quickly, they might even overlook the request.

Making the Pitch

Date: Mon, 28 Mar
Subject: I just wanted to say . . .

Hi Dr. Phelan,

I was a student in your LS2 class last quarter, and I just wanted to say that your class really impacted me. The information that I learned was valuable in itself, but beyond that, your teaching style/philosophy really inspired me. I was especially struck by what you said on the last day of lecture. You told us (though I might be poorly paraphrasing) that it was important for us as individuals to become interesting people, first and foremost—not just people rushing to get M.D. degrees because that's what our parents insist we do. (As a premed, I am familiar with that sort of pressure.) I'm truly grateful for that advice, because it made me question myself and the way I've viewed my education for the past 19 years of my life: simply as a pathway to a career that (I hope) will bring financial stability later on.

To be honest, I really wanted to get to know you and take advantage of the opportunities that you gave us to know you on a more personal level (i.e., lunches after lectures, office hours). However, for some reason or another, I just couldn't work up the . . . courage (?) to talk to you . . . so I never went to the lunches or office hours. I guess I was a bit intimidated by you and how knowledgeable/interesting of a person you seemed to be. I felt like I wouldn't have anything interesting to say and that I would simply be wasting your time. Even though I'm technically an "adult" now, I still find it hard to converse comfortably with "real adults." But . . . I really want to change that, especially after going through your class. I don't want to be a boring person for the rest of my life, passively accepting what other people say without trying to discover things for myself.

If it's okay, would I still be able to drop by your office and talk to you, even though I'm no longer enrolled in your class? (Also, if so, when would be a convenient time?) Although I'm still rather intimidated, I feel like if I don't take this step, I'll forever regret it. I don't want to sound like a suck-up, but I genuinely feel like I can learn a lot from you in terms of becoming the person that I would like to be.

One last thing—I was also interested in the research that you conducted, which you frequently referenced in class. I was wondering, are you conducting any current research? And is there any possibility that I could become involved?

Thank you so much for your time, and everything else.

–CS

Q: What are the strengths of this letter?
The tone here is nice. It's a personal letter, revealing a clear picture of the writer's personality. It feels honest, conveying vulnerability without too much insecurity. And the sentences are well written, varying in length, construction, and style, with careful and interesting word choices.

Q: Can you improve it?
The inquiry for a research position here feels a bit vague and general. It could benefit from more specificity. *Which* research mentioned in class seemed interesting? And why? Perhaps it would be better to make this request in a subsequent note.

Making the Pitch—Crashing and Burning

Dear Dr. Phelan,

I wish to apply for a research position in ecology, environmental remote sensing or hydrology in your group. Currently I am studying Ecology at Yunnan University, a famous "211" university in China.

My research scope ranges from wetlands hydrological modelling, water management to ecological effect analysis in landscape scale. With four years of study in biology and ecology as well as one year of research working, I accumulated strong ecological fieldwork experience and be [sic] skillful at geographic information system (GIS), remote sensing technical application.

As you can see from my curriculum vitae, I have been most fortunate in my college study to have obtained a wide range of research experience, both in national and provincial projects. I received the Excellent Student scholarship in Yunnan University in 2017 and 2019, respectively.

"I established myself," quote [sic] Confucius. However, I would like to establish myself further. I actively strive to enhance my research through professional programs in my interested areas. A cheerful disposition, optimistic can-do attitude, and high motive interpersonal ability [sic] make me a qualified candidate and I am certain that my academic experience and background will add value to your institute.

I am enclosing my Curriculum Vitae, which includes the detailed information of my previous qualifications, certifications, and publications. Please let me know if I can provide additional info in support of my application.

Sincerely, Tony L

Q: How many reasons are there for this letter's failure?
There are about five or six important flaws in this note, several grave enough to make failure likely.

1. The note opens abruptly without any context. Always make time for explaining who you are and why I might be interested in reading your note.
2. If there's a chance I might not be familiar with something—for example, a "211 university"—play it safe and give an explanation.
3. The research interests Tony describes are not even closely related to the person to whom he is writing. This suggests that he has fired this letter off to many people rather than to JP specifically.
4. Including a quotation isn't a bad idea. It can make for an intriguing opening to a paragraph. But the sentence is awkwardly constructed and grammatically incorrect.
5. "I am certain that my academic experience and background will add value to your institute." This is confusing because I am not part of any "institute." Again, this makes me suspicious that the letter has not been written specifically for one recipient.

Making the Pitch

Date: Thu, 6 Dec
Subject: Hi Prof. Phelan: undergrad research asst.

Hi Prof. Phelan,

You probably don't remember me at all. My name is Rishi P and I was a student in your LS2 class during Winter 2016—I had lunch with you a few times, too. I'm contacting you because I'm wondering if you are doing any sort of research, and if you are, would you be willing to take me as an undergrad research assistant. I contacted you before last year around this time, but sadly you said you had nothing available.

Throughout the years at UCLA here, I still believe you are the most easy to get along with professor—that and you are one of the best lecturers. I have a hard time staying awake with a good night's rest in some of my classes, but even with minimal sleep I was awake during yours because they were engaging—also easy to learn from.

It would be an honor to assist you. I promise I won't disappoint.

Sincerely, Rishi P

Q: What are the strengths of this letter?
This is a concise and polite letter. Rishi reminds the professor of their previous interactions, makes his request clearly, and offers a bit of praise.

Q: Can you improve it?
Hearing that a student can't stay awake in his classes isn't a good indicator about his potential quality as a research collaborator. Also, with a bit more information about why he seeks a position with this specific professor, Rishi could improve his pitch. Similarly, it might help if he could explain more of the rationale why he is seeking a research position in the first place. The opening is also a bit more negative than it needs to be.

Making the Pitch

Dear Dr. Phelan,

My name is Parvin and I was a student in your LS1 class this quarter. I just want to thank you for a great class. I thought your lectures were really interesting and I never missed a single one. (That's an achievement for me!) To be honest with you I wasn't really looking forward to taking the class; I heard from my roommates how tedious all the memorization would be. But,

I was really impressed with the way you taught the class—it was a challenge, but I feel that I learned some very valuable things that I can use for the rest of my life. Also, I really appreciate your genuine interest in student learning.

I love the sciences, but I've been a little discouraged by how all the science teachers here seem to care very little about the students. Your class was really refreshing, and helped me to remember why I'm a biology major. So, thanks again, and I would like to express interest in participating in any research you may be conducting in the near future (I'm the short girl who came up to you at your last office hour). Please contact me if you have any use for me. Thanks!

Sincerely, Parvin

P.S. By the way, I finished *Mean Genes* last week. I loved it. It raised a lot of questions for me that I'd really like to discuss with you, if you have the time. After reading it, I realize how great it was that you brought your experience and insight into a class like LS1! I don't think I would have appreciated the "march through the phylogenies" nearly as much if it weren't for all your unique examples. :)

Nicely done, Parvin. The tone, specificity, and clear, interesting writing make this a very good note.

Alita M understands the elements of a good letter, too. Read on.

The Long-Game Never Ends

Subject: Thank you!

Dear Professor Phelan,

Thank you so much for writing me a letter of recommendation to medical school, it has certainly paid off! I currently have been accepted to UCLA, UCSF, USC, UConn, and Harvard! I know that your letter definitely helped me and I really appreciate how eager you were to write it for me in spite of all the other things you have going on!

Also, I would like you to know that you are the reason I ended up applying to Harvard. Before we talked about it, I thought that I wasn't really Harvard material. "Nobody gets in to Harvard" my friends all said, and so I figured that I was better off just being happy with my west coast options. Your encouragement to apply to Harvard and your enthusiasm for the opportunities that presented themselves during your education there made me want to apply. And here I am now with the chance to attend!

While I am still deciding which school is right for me, I would like to sincerely thank you for your help. I'm sure that your letter was a big reason why I have found success at so many schools! You have been an inspiration to me as a scientist who is able to apply the principles to everyday life. I hope your book is moving along and is getting ready to inspire countless young minds like me!

Sincerely, Alita M

The Long-Game Never Ends

From: Amy W
Subject: Thank you—from a former student

Dear Dr. Phelan,

I know that you do not remember me, but I took your LS1 course 8 years ago at UCLA. I was a first-year student, trying to figure out my major. I always enjoyed biology in high school, but was hesitant to pursue it further in college. I took your course Spring

Quarter (I believe in 2011) and realized that biology is my passion. Your class captivated me and intrigued me beyond belief. I bought your *Mean Genes* book and read it cover to cover in a couple days. Your lecture style made it so easy to understand and learn in biology in a way that was never taught in high school. I graduated in 2014 with my degree in biology.

I am writing because my students (I teach high school now) just took their AP Biology exam yesterday and I was reflecting today on how I got here and who helped me along the way. I absolutely love being an AP Biology teacher. I love being able to reach out to these students and give them real life examples. I just received an educator's note saying that you have published a textbook *What is Life?* and I thought it was time to finally send you a note to thank you. I find myself referencing all the unifying concepts and themes you taught all the time in my lectures. I have told both my biology and AP biology students that biology is more than just facts on a page, and I try to get them to see the world the way that you inspired us to see it in that LS1 course.

Your teaching style truly inspired me to pursue my passion of teaching, because I felt confident that I could get people excited about science. I am constantly trying to pursue further challenges as well. I am considering a Master's degree now in biology, and I will be conducting research this summer at Cal State Fullerton to see if this is really something I want to pursue.

I am excited to review your textbook with my colleagues. Thank you again for inspiring me to be a biology major and making me want to teach.

Sincerely, Amy W

B## High School—Biology and AP Biology

**Q: Will Alita M and Amy W ever need anything else?
Will they have an ally helping them get things?**
One word: yes!

*It's Valuable to Have Professors Out There Who
Will Be Happy for the Opportunity to Help You*

> Subject: Former LS4 Student touching base
>
> Hi,
>
> You probably don't remember me, I took your LS4 (Genetics) class several years ago as an undergrad and since I was doing well in the class, I didn't come to many office hours. (In retrospect, I realize that choice was foolish.) I just wanted to let you know that you made LS4 one of my favorite classes at UCLA. I remember it as one of the classes that I always looked forward to attending. It was especially interesting for me personally since I am biracial and you gave that cool lecture on symmetry and genetics. Since then I've always been curious to see how symmetrical I am! As a result of your class, I became even more interested in genetics and took several more classes in the topic as elective courses.
>
> I'm currently in Madagascar working as a Peace Corps Volunteer. I occasionally meet up with some of the researchers here who are doing population sampling with the lemurs (and usually arguing whether to split or join different species/subspecies). It's nice to have had a class at UCLA that prepared me to help them in their work. Some people are working on studying digit proportions in lemurs, but thus far no symmetry studies. At this point I'm more worried about the preservation of the animals and plants that I love, so the projects I get involved in are more on the conservation end of things.

Anyways, I hope you are doing well. Keep up the good work as one of the few professors who takes the teaching side of their job to heart.

Ali B, Peace Corps Madagascar, B.S. UCLA, Biology

Making the Recommendation Request

Dr. Phelan,

My name is Fatima M. I was a student in your Life Science 2 class last winter. Though it was last year, it still stands as my favorite class I have taken here at UCLA, and I want to thank you again for your wonderful teaching skills. I am writing this note to inform you that I recently had an interview for a research position here on campus, and mentioned you as one of my professor references. I understand that you have many students, and may not remember us all very well, but I am sure many of them use you as a reference because you are one of few professors who reaches out to students so effectively. I apologize if I am inconveniencing at all, but I just wanted to let you know that Dr. Linda N may be contacting you regarding my performance in your class. I dropped by your office this morning, but you were not there. I will be sure to come by next week, and in the meantime, I will leave you with some information in case you are contacted. I also apologize for not asking for permission to use your name in advance.

I frequently attended your office hours, came to one of your professor lunches, and sent you a few notes about some outside research that I thought might interest you. You also lent a copy of your book to me and a group of my friends who also took the class. You asked us for an interesting and irrelevant fact about ourselves at the lunch I attended, I believe I told you that I have an unhealthy obsession with dresses, and you proceeded to tell me that your wife never wears anything other than dresses or skirts (that was just so maybe you can try to remember me!). I am also from New York, and I remember you saying how much you love to go there to write. I received an A in your class, which I hope will allow you to pass on a good word for me! I am currently a third year Physiological Sciences major, and plan to attend medical school after I graduate. I volunteer at the hospital, and am involved a great deal on campus.

Thank you so much, and I apologize again for the last-minute note. I still have your copy of *Mean Genes,* so I will be sure to bring it by your office next week. If you need any other information, please let me know.

Have a great weekend, Fatima M

THE NUTS AND BOLTS OF
LEARNING AND PERFORMING

HOW TO STUDY

(The Lessons You Need but Never Got)

Like clockwork, this message arrives shortly after the first exam is returned:

> Hello Professor,
>
> This is Aida from your Life Science class. I just saw my score on my midterm and it is horrible. I would accept it if I thought it was an accurate representation of my time in your class, but I can't begin to tell you how hard I studied for the midterm. My grade does not reflect the amount of effort and quality, diligent time spent carefully studying for the exam.
>
> I have not missed a lecture or a discussion, and I have stayed on top of my reading as well as studying for quizzes. I studied extremely hard and I felt confident that I did well on the exam. I am scared because I feel like everything I am currently putting towards preparing for the next exam still will not be good enough to do me any justice.

This may be the single most common message that we receive from students. It comes in many varieties, but the message is the same: "I was shocked by my grade because I studied so much and because I knew the material so well." Aida's assertion can be translated into, "The exam was unfair. I know my ability is better than my exam grade indicates."

While this reaction to a bad outcome is common, it is not universal. For example, consider how the swimmer Michael Phelps reacted to one of his rare Olympic disappointments. Phelps has won a total of eighteen Olympic gold medals, twice as many as the second highest total of any other athlete since the beginning of the modern Olympic Games in 1896. To be twice as successful as the second-best athlete in more than a century is remarkable.

Nonetheless, not every race has gone well for Michael Phelps. In the 2012 London Olympics, Phelps lost badly in the 400-meter individual medley. Four years earlier, in the 2008 Beijing Olympics, Phelps had been the gold medal winner in this event; in 2012, he still was the world record holder. Yet he swam slower than several other swimmers and failed to earn any medal.

Here is what Michael Phelps could have said,

> Dear Olympic Organizers, I just saw my time on the 400 IM and it is horrible. I would accept it if I thought it was an accurate representation of my training, but I can't begin to tell you how hard I worked for this race. My fourth place finish does not reflect the amount of effort and quality, diligent time spent carefully preparing for the race.
>
> I have not missed a single day of practice, and I have been on top of my weightlifting as well. I feel like everything I am currently putting toward my next event will still not be good enough to do me any justice.

What did Michael Phelps actually do?

He congratulated the winner and he blamed himself, saying simply that his performance was "horrible." A journalist even offered Phelps an excuse by asking if the outside lane with more waves and reduced visibility contributed. Phelps replied, "The lane draw had nothing to do with me coming in fourth."

Aida's surprise in her note is absolutely genuine. But it reflects two incorrect assumptions. First is that her grade should reflect how much time she spent studying. And second is that her *perception* of how well she knew the material accurately reflects how well she *actually* knew the material.

Unfortunately, both of these assumptions are wrong. These assumptions are also not unique to Aida. They are widely shared and detrimental to performance. Many students are surprised by their academic performance. And often this surprise comes when the class is over and it is too late to improve. Students often believe their outcome was unfair, the product of bad luck, bad grading, or some combination.

But our message here is not that students are delusional. On the contrary, after spending long hours studying and devoting great effort to performing well, it is reasonable to be surprised and disappointed by an unexpectedly poor outcome. In this chapter, we're going to reveal how you can prevent this from happening to you.

Here's one of the oddest things about education. We go to school to learn and from the earliest years in school we are given materials, lectures, learning activities, tests, and more. But it is rare for anyone to actually teach us how to study and learn.

Disastrously, because the general process of studying and learning isn't typically part of the specific content of any one course, it often slips through the cracks. So, we receive little guidance as to how best to study and learn. Worse, our instincts typically lead us astray, as Aida found.

Mistake #1: Read. Reread. Highlight. Listen.

The methods for studying and learning that most students discover on their own have one feature in common: they are passive. Kick your feet up on your desk and *read* the textbook. Or pull out a yellow marker and *highlight* some or all of the words on the page.

Alternatively, before class, print out pages and pages of the instructor's material that will be used during lecture. *Read* those as you listen to the professor lecture. Later, pull out your yellow marker and *highlight* some or all of those words. And, if you're really motivated, *do all this again*. Or even a third time, logging dozens of hours in "study" each week.

Mistake #2: Never Assess Your Learning

With these study methods, when the exam arrives you feel that you know the material well because everything looks familiar. Extremely familiar. But you are confusing *recognition* of the material with *mastery* of the material.

With the methods just described you won't learn that you don't actually know the material. That message comes only when you perform poorly on an exam or assignment. And that's not the best time to get that information, is it?

Six Steps to More Effective Studying

In college, the goal of studying is twofold: 1) learning, and 2) performing well when you are assessed through exams and other assignments. For maximum effectiveness, your plan for studying must incorporate several essential elements.

- Replace passive strategies with active learning.
- Rehearse material in the specific ways that you'll need to use it.

- Schedule your study sessions for maximum learning.
- Evaluate what you know and don't know.

Guided by these essential elements—and distilling decades of the published evidence from educational research—we've put together a plan for you to implement these elements in six steps to more effective studying.

Remember, you need not be alone in this planning. Judith, a friend of ours, worked in the study center of a university for years. When we asked her, "what is the one change you would make in students' behavior?" she responded with, "come and see me sooner."

These six steps will work, but so will you. (We don't want to sugarcoat reality). Still, our goal here is not for you to study more and it's not for you to study harder. It is for you to study *smarter*.

1. Take Your Own Notes

What should professors say when their students ask for written copies of the lecture notes? Before we get to the answer, consider the case of a two-year-old child addicted to smoking. A video of the child smoking surfaced, and it was so inflammatory that journalists descended on the family. They demanded to know why the father provided cigarettes to his two-year-old. In response, the father said, "He cries and throws tantrums when we don't let him smoke."

"No" is an important part of a parent's vocabulary. The desires of children, unfettered, lead to very bad outcomes. Typically, children ask for candy rather than cigarettes, but the issue is the same. The older, more experienced person must foresee the bad outcome and say no.

Written versions of the professor's lecture are the candy of college studying. However, whereas most parents say no to candy, many professors say yes. By providing written summaries of lectures, professors are freed up to deliver more content than they could when they had to write everything down on the chalkboard or projector screen (and wait for students to take notes on all of that).

In response to this increased volume of content in class, students ask their professors to make the content available, with the reasonable-sounding plea: "If we don't have to write so fast, we can focus on what you're saying without missing anything." Professors often give in to this request, but it is like allowing your children to eat candy for all of their meals: it leads to a bad outcome. So, even if they offer you the candy of posted lecture notes, don't take it.

Here's why: In carefully controlled studies, researchers have compared students' exam performance when they were given the notes by the instructor versus when the students had to take the notes themselves.

The outcome is dramatic: When generating their own notes, students score higher. In one representative study, they scored eighteen percent better! It's important to observe, too, that when forced to take their own notes, the students (whose performance increased) still reported that they were less able to focus on the instructor.

This is a disappointing message, one that you probably want to reject or ignore. We understand. We've both taken classes requiring extensive note-taking as well as classes for which the notes were given to us by the professor. Taking notes is hard!

In fact, some researchers have actually quantified just how hard it is. They did this by measuring "cognitive effort." (This is measured as the degree of interference that performing it causes in completing a secondary task.) Note-taking requires more than double the cognitive effort of simply reading sentences. In fact, it requires more cognitive effort than for an expert playing chess!

We already know it's hard to take notes. But why is *taking* notes so much better than *having* notes? We know the answer to this important question. The high cognitive effort required when taking notes activates brain processes involved in learning and memory. This, unfortunately, doesn't happen when you're just reading along with the course notes.

The educational research offers even further insights. When taking notes, students also become more attentive to numerous important signals that aid in comprehension and more active engagement in the class. Even taking into account the time pressure of note-taking and the coordination of listening, comprehending, and note production, listening alone just isn't as effective as listening with note-taking.

Here's one more finding about note-taking that you may not like. In an important research study at Princeton, researchers compared the learning of students taking notes with pen and paper to those using laptops. Notes from students using laptops were almost verbatim transcripts of the lecture. Students using pen and paper were slower, resulting in fewer notes. Rather than reducing their learning, however, the physical note-taking required those students to engage more deeply with the material, so that they could summarize the ideas.

In a subsequent test of their learning, both groups performed equally on questions requiring simple factual recall. For conceptual questions, however, those who took notes by hand performed significantly better (by about one-third of a standard deviation).

No pain, no gain. We can't make it easier, but maybe you can take some solace from a bit of former bodybuilder Arnold Schwarzenegger's wisdom about pain:

> *The only way to be a champion is by going through these forced reps and the torture and pain. That's why I call it the torture routine. Because it's like forced torture. Torturing my body. What helps me is to think of this pain as pleasure. Pain makes me grow. Growing is what I want. Therefore, for me, pain is pleasure. And so, when I am experiencing pain I'm in heaven. It's great. People suggest this is masochistic. But they're wrong. I like pain for a particular reason. I don't like needles stuck in my arm. But I do like the pain that is necessary to be a champion.*

"No pain, no gain" is also true for our minds. Relying solely on notes written for you causes you to learn *less* in lecture.

2. Take Better Notes

Taking notes is important, but it isn't enough. Terry had a student, Bahiti, who was on the border of failing every test. Some students fail because they don't try. That was not the case for Bahiti. She came to every class, turned in every homework assignment, and, furthermore, she was the valedictorian of her high school.

One day, Bahiti inadvertently turned in her class notes rather than the problem set. This mistake was serendipitous; her notes revealed the problem.

What had Bahiti done so wrong in her notes? Did she have some incorrect ideas written down? Were her notes incomplete? No. Her notes were perfect—identical, letter-for-letter, to the lecture notes that Terry used to write on the board. Bahiti had made exactly one modification. On one page, in addition to Terry's exact text, she had drawn a single flower. The act of going to lecture for Bahiti consisted of transcribing, word for word, what Terry wrote. Nothing more, nothing less.

An old joke is that a college class is the process of transferring the professor's notes into the student's notes without any brains involved. The movie *Real Genius* carries this joke to its logical conclusion. The movie is set at Pacific Tech, a thinly disguised version of nerdy Caltech in Pasadena, California. Over the course of the movie, fewer and fewer students attend lecture. Instead, they leave behind tape recorders.

If the goal of lecture is simply to get down the professor's words, then a tape recorder is better than almost all humans. Once all the students stop coming to classes, the Pacific Tech professor also stops coming, and instead sends a tape recorder to play his lecture.

If transferring notes from the professor to the student is teaching, then providing an exact copy of the lecture is an educational advance. However, this is exactly the wrong way to enhance learning.

What makes class notes effective? The answer isn't particularly surprising. It has to do with turning note-taking into an active, rather than passive, process, and making note-taking part of your learning of the material. (Because a great deal of rigorous educational research on this question has produced unambiguous findings, we have high confidence that it is true). It should serve as a guide for your own note-taking.

- Take comprehensive and coherent notes during lectures. You're not trying to record a transcript of exactly what is said. But, when in doubt, more is better.
- Indicate a clear organization with an obvious framework. There's nothing wrong with asking your professor to put

an outline of each lecture on the board—she almost certainly created one when developing the lesson.

- Go beyond what your professor includes on slides or the board. Much of the important content and context won't be written down but will instead be spoken. Including those spoken comments in your notes is extremely valuable when you are reviewing your notes weeks or months later.

- Include critical specific details and examples, as well as connections to other topics. When learning material, it is valuable to learn how to illustrate main ideas through examples.

- Note points of particular emphasis as revealed by your professor's words, tone, and body language. Listen not just to what your professor is saying, but how she says it. Superlatives? Repetition? Red-flag words like "really" and "important" are not simple space fillers. All words are not created equal; key into the important ones and indicate this in your notebook with big stars or arrows. Body language is particularly important when it comes to detecting cues that reveal the relative importance of what they are saying. Are they gesturing more emphatically than usual? Have they stopped glancing down at their notes to look right at the class?

Finally, because it takes so much focus and effort to record high-quality notes, you will also want to recopy and refine your notes after class. Use this version in your studying. The exercise of recopying and refining your notes significantly improves your learning and your future note-taking.

Here's a useful guide. The notes you take in class should allow your roommate—who is not enrolled in the class—to understand fully what happened in the class. If you ever wonder whether your notes are as effective as they could be, just try that test.

3. Use "Elaborative Interrogation"
(Translation: Study by Writing and Answering Questions)

During graduate school, our friend Ashish went to a seminar that we were unable to attend. Afterward, Terry asked him, "What was the speaker's main point?" Ashish described what the speaker talked about, but Terry wasn't satisfied. "I don't mean, 'what did he say?' I mean, 'What was his main point?'"

Ashish then described (in remarkable detail) what the speaker's words had been. But it became clear that he couldn't articulate the actual *point* the speaker was trying to make (and they are not the same thing). If you are able to tell someone only that "we talked about Mendel in class—you know, wrinkled peas and genetics," you haven't conveyed even a single idea.

For this reason, although organized, clear, and beautiful notes are crucial, they're not enough. That's why you will benefit from turning your notes into a more powerful learning tool by creating a "question list."

> Come up with twenty to thirty questions from each day's lecture notes. Use a separate notebook. (5 × 7 index cards are even better.) Begin with the small stuff. Ask for definitions of new terms introduced. Ask for descriptions of the examples given to illustrate each idea.

Don't worry about the fact that you're not an expert at writing questions. Your purpose here is not to generate new knowledge. You are creating your own sort of *Jeopardy!* quiz show.

Your notes represent all the answers, and you've just got to write questions for which that information is the answer. Leave nothing out. Memorizing often gets a bad rap. But it's a helpful, even necessary, part of learning. After you've covered all the smaller stuff, write some "main point" questions. (If the main point isn't clear, you'll need to ask the instructor.)

Later, using just your question list, write the answers down. Don't just do this in your head. *Write* the answers. Then check them against your class notes, the textbook, and any other relevant course materials. Correct any vagueness or sloppiness—in writing—within your answer. Complete this for all of your questions. Later, when it gets closer to an exam date, do it again. Think of writing and rewriting your answers as rehearsing for your exam.

Ideally, you will spend the majority of your studying time working on this practice of "elaborative interrogation." Evidence from rigorous research studies revealed that students using the "elaborative interrogation" method of studying performed about forty percent better on their final exams than did students who only read and reread their notes. This is huge.

Rehearsal strategies such as elaborative interrogation are effective. It can, however, feel overwhelming to add an additional time-consuming activity to your studying regime. So, don't just add it to your usual study habits. Instead, it is worth evaluating ways to reduce your time spent on less effective, passive studying techniques—such as rereading and highlighting texts—to free up time for this more valuable practice. If necessary, just start small with this strategy and gradually reapportion your study time as you see its effectiveness.

4. Focus on Practice Tests, Not "Restudying"
Performance. Feedback. Revision. Performance. Feedback. Revision . . .

Improvement in any task requires assessment and correction. Evaluation and revision. This is true whether you're learning to snowboard—where the feedback may be as simple as a face-plant in the snow—or calculus.

In order to improve your knowledge and understanding, you must identify your weaknesses and improve on them. Aida, the student who wrote the note at the beginning of this chapter, never got feedback as she went about her studying. As a result, she was lulled into a false sense of security based on the fact that she *recognized* all the material.

If Aida had, instead, devoted time to practicing answering meaningful and relevant questions about the material, and getting feedback from her professor or teaching assistant or classmates, she would have gotten a harsh wake-up call: she had not actually mastered the material. Ultimately, she did get that wake-up call when she saw her midterm score. But it would have been much better if she got that information sooner and without hurting her grade.

There are many ways to get feedback: practicing with old exams from your instructor, using online quizzes and assigned problem sets, studying questions from the textbook, and going over other course materials. Quizzing yourself with the questions that you and your classmates write for each other (that we suggested in the previous study tip) is particularly effective.

Find out from your instructor what types of questions you will be asked on your exams: multiple-choice, short-answer, page-long essays, longer essays, etc. Then test your ability to demonstrate your mastery of the material using those exact types of questions.

Suppose you joined a track and field team to become a pole-vaulter. You might read some books on pole-vaulting. You might watch some videos about pole-vaulting. And you might get instructions from a coach. Nonetheless, if you know that your performance in a meet will be evaluated by your actual pole-vaulting ability (and it will), you should actually practice pole-vaulting! Right?

Similarly, if you are going to be evaluated on your ability to write one-page essays about psychology, the first time you ever write one page essays about psychology should NOT be at the actual exam. Instead, you should have written dozens and dozens of practice answers in that format prior to the exam. Similarly, if your exam is multiple-choice questions exclusively, you should have answered as many multiple-choice questions as possible in preparation.

Hundreds of research studies have evaluated the value of using practice tests versus restudying. The overwhelming finding is that practice testing results in a significant improvement on final exam performance, typically thirty percent or more. Importantly, this finding is consistent regardless of whether the final exams primarily test basic facts or more complex concepts.

Whatever the source of the practice questions, however, the benefit is increased by getting feedback on your performance. This can include comparing your answers with those from solutions guides or posted answer keys. You can also get them from your instructors. Show them what you've done, have them evaluate your work, and ask them to show you how you could improve. Then try again. Find out what you don't know *before* your exam.

5. Interleave the Material Rather than Blocking

It's common practice for students to focus on a single topic during a study session. This method of studying is called "blocking." It includes solving all of the practice problems of one type before moving on to the next material. An alternative method—

called "interleaving"—is to switch between different subtopics within a course in each study session.

It can be challenging to hold the material from multiple topics in your head at the same time when studying. For this reason, if you use blocking when you are studying, your performance (on practice problems) typically is better. In one well-controlled study, researchers found that students' accuracy on practice problems was close to thirty percent higher when blocking. So it's not surprising that you might take that as evidence that blocking is always superior to interleaving. But it's not.

When course exams include material from multiple topics, students using interleaved practice score significantly better. In the same study mentioned previously, the exam scores of students using interleaving during their studying were forty percent higher than those using blocked practice. This reinforces the idea we described in the previous section: it's important to develop your ability to use your knowledge in the way you will be tested.

For this recommendation of interleaving over blocked study, we need to ask you to trust us (and the research evidence). Consider this odd finding. For different exams, students used either blocked or interleaved practice. When they were asked to judge their exam performance, more than sixty percent believed they performed better using blocked practice, while only twenty percent believed they performed better with interleaving. (The remaining students believed there was no difference.)

The actual performance of these students, however, revealed that their perceptions were wrong. Eighty percent performed better with interleaved study, and only about fifteen percent performed better with blocked practice. It's strange but true: our own beliefs about how we learn and perform best aren't necessarily correct!

6. Learn . . . Forget . . . Relearn

Spend less time studying and perform better on the exam. Can it be true? Is this just a fake claim like a weight-loss product advertising, "lose over twenty pounds in your first week"?

We are absolutely serious. You can perform better with significantly less study time. All that is required is the precious commodity of willpower.

The key is to learn how to space out your studying time. Is it good to cram your studying into a few hours before the exam? Almost never, but Terry did once suggest that a student cram. More on that in a moment.

How many hours do you need to study for a class to perform your best? It varies a lot from one class to another, of course. In any case, however, this is the wrong question to ask. For a fixed amount of studying for a class—let's say a hundred hours—the amount you learn (and how well you will retain it) depends on how those hundred study hours are spaced out.

Put simply, cramming for ten hours a day for two days leads to less learning and worse retention than dividing twenty hours across four weeks. Even if you use all the valuable strategies and techniques outlined in this chapter, this remains true.

This is called the "spacing effect" and it turns out to be one of the most consistent and well-documented phenomena in all of educational research. And it goes beyond the idea that you probably already suspected: cramming isn't the best way to learn.

For any type of learning, spacing out your studying and practicing is *much* more effective than massing your efforts in fewer, longer sessions. In fact, you'll have the best learning and long-term retention when you space out your studying so that you learn the material, then allow enough time to pass so that you forget it, and then learn it again. That's how the human brain works.

Moreover, just as we saw with the blocking versus interleaving issue, your own instincts and perceptions on this issue are misleading. Typically, your short-term performance following cramming is better when you evaluate it during studying and practice. But, when it comes to your long-term performance (think: final exams), massed study (also known as cramming!) comes up short, and not just a little bit.

The difference is huge. In numerous research studies spanning the past fifty years, long-term performance can be twice as good using spaced out study sessions—even when the total number of hours studied is identical!

So cramming is bad. Then why did Terry tell a student to cram? Here's the situation. Terry was teaching a year-long, introductory economics course. He gave out his phone number and told his students that they could call him anytime, saying, "If you are thinking about economics, I am thinking about economics."

At 2am one night, the phone rang with student Greg calling.

Terry:	Hey, Greg, What's up?
Greg:	The final is in seven hours, I am calling to get your advice on what to emphasize.
Terry:	What have you done so far?
Greg:	Nothing. I'm just getting started. (Remember this was a year-long course.)
Terry:	Usually, I tell students at this point to get some sleep. But in your case, I suggest you stay up all night and work on the following material . . .

So cramming is better than nothing. But it's still worse than almost every other way to study.

This knowledge can give you a real edge. It's like getting a free lunch: You don't have to study **more** to get better outcomes. You have to study **smarter**. The catch, however, is that you must study even when there is no looming deadline.

———————

Reading this chapter, you already know that we ask a lot from you.

- Take comprehensive and coherent notes.
- Do not use the professor's verbatim notes (even if available).
- Be active in your studying—annotate your materials, connect the content with your prior knowledge and experiences.
- Rewrite your notes.
- Write dozens of your own questions. Then write the answers.
- Examine yourself, and give yourself an "F" if that's what you deserve.
- Study in uncomfortable ways. Be tough on yourself.
- Study regularly, even when there is no imminent deadline.

At this point, you may be thinking, these professors are crazy. And we are . . . crazy like experienced foxes. We have learned what works. These are the techniques that will allow you to achieve your ambitious goals.

When it comes to studying, you can take the standard path. Slip into lecture twenty seconds before the bell with a printout of the lecture. Allow your mind to wander during class. Collect all the material so you can cram it the night before the exam. Reread the book. Contact your professor when you are surprised and disappointed with the poor test that inaccurately gave you a low score.

Or do something different. Bring some blank paper to class and several pens. Listen closely. Take rich notes. Record your thoughts, emotions, and perceptions in the margins. Embrace the rarity of your approach. Commit. Struggle. And succeed!

Take Home Messages

1. You will learn and remember your course content better if you fully focus and take your own notes during class (even if your professor makes complete class notes available to you).

2. Take comprehensive and coherent notes during lectures, beyond what your instructor includes on slides or the board. Your notes must have clear organization with an obvious framework. They must include critical specific details. And they must note points of particular emphasis as revealed by your professor's words, tone, and body language. Recopy and refine your notes after class.

3. Create comprehensive lists of questions from your class notes. Spend most of your study time by practicing writing (and revising and rewriting) concise, precise, accurate answers to your questions.

4. Use practice-testing extensively as you prepare for exams. Perfect your ability to use your knowledge in the way that you will be tested. Get accurate, expert feedback on your mastery of the course material so that you can identify where and how you need to improve.

5. Interleave sections of the material when studying rather than restricting your efforts to just one topic at a time.

6. Space out your studying. For optimum learning and long-term retention: Learn the material. Allow enough time to forget. Learn it again.

11

EXAMS

How to Perform When It Counts Most

> *It's not going to come easy. This is a [team] that's
> going to hit you. They are going to try and hit you . . .
> Just hit, just run, just block, and just tackle. You do
> that and there is no question what the outcome is
> going to be in this ball game. Keep your poise.*

—Vince Lombardi—considered one of the greatest coaches
in the history of sports—in a motivational speech before
Super Bowl II (won by Lombardi's Green Bay Packers)

Taking an exam has much in common with an athletic competition. Paraphrasing Lombardi, "It's not going to come easy. This is an exam that's going to hit you. Just think, just calculate, and just write. Keep your poise."

For college courses with exams, there are three distinct phases (as there are with sports). There is preparation. There is the exam itself. And there is the post-exam review. In this chapter, we cover exam performance, from the moment you start the exam until it is completed. Once an exam begins, your goal is to get the best grade possible *given what you know at the time of the exam*. In chapters 10 and 15, we explain how to prepare for the exam and what to do after the exam.

Test Taking Essentials

Let's first quickly review *Exam Performance 101*, those basic techniques commonly taught in the early years of school. Then we'll progress to more sophisticated strategies. The conventional wisdom is as follows:

1. Read the entire exam.
2. Answer the questions in a nonlinear path that ensures you receive all the easy points.
3. Answer every question.

A second-grade test of Terry's looked like this:

```
2ⁿᵈ Grade Math Test      Date: _____
Trombley Elementary      Name: _____
Ms. Salamis, Room 1B
```

```
Please read the entire exam before starting
work.
```

```
1)   $1.25      2)   $7.28      3)   $9.68
   – $1.00         – $3.54         – $3.43
     $ .             $ .             $ .


4)   $6.89      5)   $7.47      6)   $9.90
   – $4.55         – $4.52         – $6.57
     $ .             $ .             $ .
```

```
Write your name on the exam, put your pencil
down and wait for the teacher.

Do not do any of the math problems above.

END OF EXAM
```

A perfect score is a blank test with name and date. When this test is administered, some children follow the instructions and finish in a few minutes. Most students, however, do not read the whole exam before starting work, and thus begin completing the math problems. There are some nervous laughs as those who read the whole exam smile at each other, and laugh at those failing to comply with the directions as they work through the math problems.

This exam is amusing (or irritating) in second grade, but the teacher's point has value for college students. If possible, you should at least skim through the entire exam before beginning— even when you know that you will be time-pressed. In fact, if you expect to be pressed for time, this is even more important. Here's why.

Jay completes detailed statistical analyses of student performance on his UCLA exams. From these, he finds that students consistently leave free money on the table, in the form of unanswered or hastily answered easy questions.

In one of Jay's courses, there is a midterm exam that includes six short essay questions. Each is worth fifteen points and requires about one page of writing. Over a five-year period, this is how his students performed:

Question	Average Score
1	85%
2	73%
3	69%
4	80%
5	54%
6	42%

Do you see a pattern? Performance on the last two questions—especially the very last question—is significantly lower than for the other questions. Why might that be?

1) Maybe the last two questions are more difficult.

But it could also be that:

2) Students answer the questions in a linear sequence, with no consideration as to which questions they are best prepared for and, therefore, on which they are likely to receive the most points.

To determine the cause, Jay rearranged the question order. He found that performance on the final two questions was always lower than for the first four. And when a question was the first or second question on the exam, the average score on that question was typically thirty to forty percent better than when the identical question was made the last question. The questions with the low scores were not more difficult; their position on the exam is what caused the poor performance.

What does this mean for you? When it is possible, you should peruse the entire exam before starting. (With some computerized exams this is not possible; ask your instructor beforehand.) Prioritize the order in which you answer the questions based on your own preparation and knowledge—get the low-hanging fruit first.

Similarly, if there will be a mix of multiple choice and short answer questions, plan ahead and begin with the section which will allow you to earn the most points. If the technology allows, don't simply proceed through the exam in a linear fashion.

Grading and Exams from the Instructor's Perspective

Let's contemplate another aspect of exams—grading—that may help you approach test taking in a way that enables you to get the best possible outcomes. Before we start, what is it like to be the grader? And why do we even have grades?

For most instructors, grading exams is a time-consuming chore. Consider a class with 120 students, each of whom has completed a three-hour final exam. How long does it take to grade those exams? If the instructor took as long to grade as the students took to write the exam, it would take 360 hours—nine full 40-hour weeks! Of course, nine weeks of grading is not feasible. So, you can be confident that your exam will be graded in much less time than it took you to complete the test.

Many instructors might prefer not to give grades. However, at nearly every college, instructors are required by their school to give grades that vary. Here's a surreal story: After one year in his current job at Chapman University, Terry was chastised for awarding "grades that were too high." *Grades too high??* Chapman had previously sent Terry a letter stating that the highest average grade he could award was 2.7 out of 4.0, which translated to an average grade of B–.

Before submitting his grades, Terry calculated that he had given an average of 2.65, safely under the 2.7 limit. So why did he get in trouble? Terry had taught two separate offerings of the same course. One section had an average grade of 2.75, while the second averaged 2.55. Thus, Terry learned that the university rules required each section—not just the average across all of his students in the same course—to be below the maximum.

In most schools, instructors must perform two sometimes-conflicting tasks. First: teach. And second: assess the students' mastery of the content. This second task is typically accomplished, in part, by performance on exams. Schools vary tremendously in the proportions of students receiving each of the grades. Rarely, however, is a school happy with an instructor whose students all receive A's.

Because instructors are expected then to give a range of grades, it behooves them to write exams at a level of difficulty that is likely to produce a range of scores. Such exams provide instructors (as well as their students) with the most information about the students' relative mastery of the course content. Consider three types of questions:

1. Easy questions that are answered correctly by all students.
2. Exceedingly difficult questions that all students get wrong.
3. Intermediate-level problems, answered correctly by some students and incorrectly by others, with still others earning partial credit.

Only with questions of intermediate difficulty can instructors evaluate which students have gained a full and nuanced mastery of the content while also discriminating among students with respect to this mastery. By crafting exams in this way, instructors are able to grade exams efficiently and give fair and meaningful grades to students across differing ability levels.

Three Test-Taking Tips

1. Harvest "Low-Hanging Fruit" First

Lock in the points that you can earn most quickly and with most certainty. How do you do this? When preparing for your exams, think about the exam from the perspective of the instructor.

For most instructors the exam question topics will be hidden in plain sight from day one. The questions will be drawn directly from the lectures, the assignments, and other course material.

As you study, think of it as a game: predict the most likely exam question topics. Argue your case with your classmates. Practice writing short bits about those most-likely-to-show-up-on-the-exam topics. Afterward, referring back to your notes and other course materials, modify and improve those short answers. Then write them again.

On the exam, find the questions that cover the topics you were most certain would be addressed. For those topics, you will already have prepared, practiced, and refined your answers. Secure this "low-hanging fruit" by completing these questions immediately.

2. Be Smart—Even in Your Ignorance

During his second year at Harvard, Jay faced a big hurdle in his graduate program in biology. The "Oral Qualifying Exam" consists of three or four professors grilling you on all topics in your field for several hours. Then you wait in the hallway while they deliberate and decide your fate.

Eventually, the examiners call you back into the room and tell you the result. Passing the exam qualifies you to stay at Harvard and complete your PhD. If you fail, however, you must pack up your office and leave the program and the university. You will have to return home to your family as a failure. ("This is my son, Jay, he flunked out and now lives in his fifth-grade bedroom.") To describe the oral exam as stressful is an extreme understatement.

Having prepared for months, Jay was cautiously optimistic. This changed with the opening question. Professor Bossert said, "We'll start with an easy one. Give me a Leslie matrix that won't evolve to a stable age distribution." Wait, what?? This made as much sense to Jay as if Bossert had said, "Will you mambo dogface to the banana patch?"

Jay hemmed and hawed for several minutes, hoping for some additional clue or guidance. Or an admission from Professor Bossert that he was just kidding. No such luck. Walking to a chalkboard, Jay fell back on a strategy that can help you in similar times of panic and impending failure.

> *Well, we're looking for a matrix. It'll have some columns, let's say four of them. . . .*

> *And it'll have rows. Let's say four of them as well.*

Long pause. No assistance from the professors.

> *And, um, moving across the top of the matrix, we indicate the birth rate for each age group. And moving down the diagonal, we'd indicate the survival rate for each age category. . . .*

With all of his knowledge on the topic exhausted, Jay just sort of trailed off.

Finally, Bossert spoke: "Yes. You understand what the question is." This terse statement translates to, "the committee that decides your fate is not impressed. If you don't up your game, you can pack your bags." Bossert finally relented, saying, "Well, we won't belabor the point. Let's move on."

A better response to this Leslie Matrix question would have involved eigenvectors and application of the Euler–Lotka equation. Jay knows that now, but was not able to articulate it at the time. He could have simply given up and said, "I don't know," but that would have led to disaster.

There's no getting around the fact that Jay did not answer this question correctly. In fact, Jay didn't answer the question incorrectly either, because he was not able to even give an answer. The best thing we can say is that Jay was smart in his ignorance. And that even from his poor performance there is a lesson to be learned.

At some point, you may have your own "Leslie matrix" moment. You have no idea how to answer an important question. You aren't even equipped to make a wild guess. What you don't want to do is leave a blank space. Most instructors truly do want you to pass their exams and their courses. But you've got to give them something to work with. Perhaps the only certainty when it comes to exam performance is this:

If you write nothing, you will receive nothing.

How can you be smart about your ignorance?

1. Break down the question into any possible simpler questions.
2. Restate the question in your own words.
3. Articulate the nature of a desirable answer. Something like, "And this would be an argument that is consistent with . . ." Include, if possible, assertions on the topic that you know to be true. "The Soviet Union was created in 1917."
4. And define precisely any and all of the relevant ideas and/ or terms that would likely be part of a complete and accurate answer.

When it comes to multiple-choice exam questions for which you don't know the answers, you must apply a version of this lesson. Nudge the odds of a good score in your favor. Ruling out even one of the 'distractors' (the incorrect, but plausible, answers) has value. Ruling out two or more is hugely valuable. Over the course of a long exam, even this slight improvement in your probability of guessing correctly can be the difference between passing and failing.

3. Structure Your Answers for Easy Grading

Consider this exam question and two potential answers:

Question: *Injection of botulinum toxin (Botox) is the most common nonsurgical cosmetic procedure in the U.S. By what mechanism does Botox have its desired effects? In your answer, also describe normal signal transmission at a synapse.*

Answer A:

Botox blocks the release of acetylcholine from neurons that synapse with muscle cells, paralyzing the muscles. Specific mechanism: Botox inactivates proteins (including SNAP-25) in terminal buttons of motor neurons. These proteins are essential for causing acetylcholine-containing vesicles to bind with the presynaptic neuron membrane and release the neurotransmitter into the synapse, causing muscle contraction. Consequently, when a neuron sends a signal to the muscle to contract, acetylcholine is not released and the muscle does not contract—it is, in essence, paralyzed. After two to four months, the effect wears off.

Answer B:

Botox blocks the release of acetylcholine from neurons that synapse with muscle cells, paralyzing the muscles.

Specific mechanism:

Botox inactivates proteins (including SNAP-25) in terminal buttons of motor neurons. These proteins are essential for causing acetylcholine-containing vesicles to bind with the presynaptic neu-

ron membrane and release the neurotransmitter into the synapse, causing muscle contraction.

Consequently, when a neuron sends a signal to the muscle to contract, acetylcholine is not released and the muscle does not contract—it is, in essence, paralyzed. After two to four months, the effect wears off.

Which is better? They're the same! Right? Or maybe they're not . . . These two answers should (and would!) get different grades. The first isn't terrible, but would you really want to grade it? (We're willing to bet that you didn't/couldn't even read it fully and skimmed it instead.) Why is the second answer more appealing?

There's no way around it. For even the most devoted and motivated teachers, grading is hard work. It's slow, cognitively taxing, and exhausting. As a student, however, it is within your power to make the task considerably easier for the grader, and thereby increase your score.

When taking an exam, make it as easy as possible for the grader to see that you have answered all parts of the question and have done so precisely and concisely. Using this process, you'll usually increase not just the number of points you *deserve* but also the number of points you *receive*. The approach requires very little effort, but can have a huge benefit.

To ensure your exam answers are more effective and easier to grade, consider doing these three things:

- **Use boxes around definitions.** To the side of your answer, define any terminology that is specific to the subject of the course. You're separating them from the rest of your answer—like a footnote—so that you don't disrupt the flow of your answer with a side-trip to definition-land. Putting a box around it allows them to see at a glance that you have a tight grasp of the subject's special lexicon.

- **Don't neglect making appropriate paragraph breaks—with clear space between them—in your answer.** Don't devise a scavenger hunt that requires your teacher to seek out the treasures in giant paragraphs. It is more valuable than usual to communicate effectively when conveying your mastery of ideas in an exam.

- **Use numbered sequences of thoughts to step logically through the parts of your answer.** Yes, you can even set up your answer as a linear sequence of ideas and examples. The numbers break up your answer into discrete, manageable chunks. This makes them appealing to read and evaluate. Numbers can be preferable to bullet points because they call attention to the fact that there is a *progression* of arguments rather than a laundry list of facts. But including the bullet list is usually preferable to the long, run-on paragraph.

Take Home Messages

1. If possible, read or skim an entire exam before beginning to answer. Complete the exam in a nonlinear fashion after prioritizing your time, in order to maximize the number of points you get.

2. Instructors are looking for objective ways to evaluate students' differences—even subtle ones—in their mastery of the course content. Grading is laborious; exams are designed to be graded both efficiently and (one hopes) fairly.

3. Make sure to get the points you most deserve. Do this by anticipating which ideas, concepts, and issues are most certain to be on the exam. Find them and secure those points first.

4. Be smart—even in your ignorance. When you encounter exam questions which you have no idea how to answer, keep in mind that your instructors can give you partial credit only if you give them something to work with. This includes writing accurate statements that convey that you have made an effort to learn the content and to convey some of that knowledge.

5. For short-answer and essay questions, make it as easy as possible for the grader to see that you have answered all parts of the question precisely and concisely. Employ graphical devices, paragraph breaks, spacing, and design elements to guide the grader to and through your answer.

PAPERS AND OTHER WRITING ASSIGNMENTS

Say It Better

The *Worst-Case Scenario Survival Handbook* includes a section on "How to Escape from Killer Bees."

- Run away; swatting at bees only makes them angrier. Run through bushes or high grass.
- Remove the stinger by raking your fingernail across it in a sideways motion.
- Do not jump into a lake or swimming pool.

The survival handbook's detailed advice covers a wide range of extreme scenarios. Escaping from quicksand? Winning a sword fight? Defusing a bomb? Delivering a baby in a taxicab? They've got you covered. If your particular peril isn't one of the forty they address, however, you're on your own.

We face a similar conundrum in dispensing guidance for completing college assignments. The dozens of different types of college assignments include mathematical problem sets, artistic sketches, works of fiction, dance performances, production of videos and films, verbal debates, research papers, and many more.

Because we can't hope to give specific advice on every type of assignment, we'll restrict our focus to college papers and writing assignments, with an eye toward more general writing tips and guidance.

———————————

During his Marine Corps armor crewman training (also known as "Tank School"), Terry was named the "Marine of the Cycle." This was the highest honor possible, awarded to the best Marine in a class of 100 students. Along with this honor and a promotion in rank from Private First Class to Lance Corporal, Terry acquired a valuable approach to success.

Tank School included performance tasks and written tests covering a wide range of tasks and knowledge—shooting the main tank gun, disassembling and rebuilding a pistol, knowing the speed of an anti-tank round, etc. A single failure on any evaluation made a candidate ineligible for the "Marine of the Cycle" award.

You've likely heard this sort of talk in movies: "Whisky Tango Foxtrot, this is Alpha Six actual, providing coordinates for an artillery strike after code verification. Over." This military language is taught and tested in tank school.

When the time came for the exam, Terry happened to be in the middle of the line as each Marine was assessed individually. Several of the Marines emerged and noted (inappropriately) that the examiner failed people based on their pronunciation of the letter Q.

In the military alphabet, A is Alpha, B is Bravo, etc., and Q is Quebec, as in the province of Canada. This particular instructor required Marines to pronounce the Q without a "w" sound. So, whereas the dictionary lists the pronunciation as "kwi BEK," passing the Tank School communications test required removing the 'w' to yield, "ki BEK."

Armed with this seemingly trivial knowledge, Terry passed the test, remained in the eligible pool for Marine of the Cycle, and went on to eventual victory.

Is the take home message to cheat and find out what is on the test in advance? No. It is that every assessment is created and administered by human beings—people (usually experts) with particular beliefs about the most important material. In this case, the communications test creator believed that mispronouncing Quebec might lead to confusion and death in combat. Hence, the assessment put tremendous emphasis on this one part of the material that had been taught.

The message for students is to invest some time to (legally) determine what is most important to the instructor and grader. Usually, this information is obvious from the course; sometimes it is not.

One solid approach is to speak to the instructor after the first assignment. Preface your request by making it clear that you are interested in improving your future performance and not angling to change your previous grade. A second approach is to review assignments from previous offerings of the instructor's course. Also, pay careful attention to cues from the instructor, such as from printed instructions, subtle reactions to in-class questions, and discussions.

During a particularly challenging semester, Jay fell behind in a lab course. In order to finish his work for another class, he neglected the lab course and did not complete one of the lab reports.

The syllabus specified that your course grade would be based on your performance on five lab reports. Specifically, it said,

"Each lab report is worth 20 points. They must be turned in during class on the day they are due. One point will be deducted for each day late."

By the time Jay had caught up with his other courses, the lab report due date was two weeks passed. After doing the math, Jay decided it wouldn't be worth it to turn in a report at that point. Even if the lab report was perfect, he wouldn't be able to get a passing grade.

When the course teaching assistant asked about the lab report, Jay simply said that it wasn't going to be worth it to do the work. (He even felt perversely clever for recognizing the futility of attempting the missing lab report.) Jay assumed that the rules were all that mattered when it came to the instructor's evaluation of his performance in the class.

This was exactly the wrong approach to take. Obviously, you should do everything you can to complete your assigned work. Remember, however, that instructors are human and they care about your commitment to their course. Your instructors understand that students are people too, and that people mess up. They want to help you, but it's up to you to give them justification to provide that help.

Choosing to not do the work is like a slap in their face, an active rejection of their efforts to give you something of educational value. Even if it isn't an official part of their rubric, they will value the signals you send (or don't send) of caring and effort.

Before the term ended, Jay should have completed and submitted the lab report. He could have apologized and explained his regret at missing the deadline, making it clear he knew he had lost most (or all) of the possible points. Then he could convey that he gained valuable knowledge from the class and still would appreciate any feedback on his work that the instructor might be able to give him.

Specific Methods for Effective Writing

So far, we've given you some big picture advice to help you approach your assignments: 1) pay close attention to the "rules" of the assignments; 2) be aware of the specific audience grading the assignments and their particular perspective on the content; 3) never lose sight of the fact that the evaluator of your performance is human and likely cares about your effort and progress.

When it comes to "the little picture," it's harder to give universally applicable advice. Assignments and paper topics differ, and so do the people grading them. Similarly, there isn't one standard, correct writing style for every student and situation. Nonetheless, at least three general practices turn out to be almost essential to effective writing.

1. Use a Methodical, Comprehensive Approach to Preparing and Writing a Paper

Shortcuts will make writing take longer. You may have procrastinated until the last minute, but that only makes this rule more valuable to you. Don't just start typing, adding words until you run out of steam and hoping that your stream of consciousness will yield coherent output. No matter what the assignment is, you will benefit from a methodical approach with specific goals.

Brainstorm about potential ideas for your paper.

Consider why your instructor created this particular assignment. It wasn't an accident. How does it fit in with other readings, class discussions, and the central themes of the course?

As you narrow your list, if there is time and opportunity, speak with your instructor. But be specific in articulating why you are considering each idea and approach. Have clear and concise explanations for your choices and any potential challenges you foresee.

This is also a good time to ask about relevant sources. Make it clear you have done some of the initial legwork. Listen carefully, so that you can benefit from your professor's expertise—both in identifying valuable sources and in narrowing and clarifying your ideas.

Proceed to the next step only when you have a topic and angle on it that is relevant and interesting to you, and which has been vetted by your instructor.

Compile your ideas and information in one "All stories and data" file.

Write and/or cut-and-paste into a single file, all of the information that you might use to draft your paper. This may be excerpts from sources: original published papers, a specific text you may be focusing on, your own ideas and analyses, questions to address, etc. Don't worry about the organization at this point. Just get everything in one place.

Identify your three or four Take Home Messages.

Articulate clearly, in three or four succinct statements, your main points. This is the time to hone your ideas and confirm that you have something nonobvious to say. After you've developed these, reading through them should feel like a clear and succinct executive summary of your paper.

Create an outline.

OK, your eyes probably glaze over when you see, "Create an outline." But don't feel obligated to think of this as a formal step. Do it on the back of an envelope if that makes it seem less of a tedious task. Just sketch out a broad road map. You'll know that you are ready to begin writing if you can give a precise and concise "elevator pitch" of the idea. Try it on your roommates or friends if they'll listen.

Start writing.

It helps if you can approach your paper as a series of smaller, more manageable sections, each serving to support a clear Take Home Message (regardless of whether that THM is stated explicitly). Incorporate the facts, examples, and stories earmarked for each section. Be ruthless in this process: include an idea or fact or story *only* if it clearly supports your Take Home Message for the section you are writing.

Don't feel obligated to write the sections of your paper in the order they will appear. It can be revealing, for example, to start with the last paragraph or section. Where do you ultimately arrive in your arguments? Can you fill in the story, working backward one section at a time, illuminating how you came to understand and believe the ideas you articulate?

Finally, be original. Whatever you choose to write about, make it your own. You may address and consider ideas presented in class or found online, but make sure that the core ideas of your presentation are your own.

2. Revisions Are the Key to Writing

Mozart is among the top two or three most popular composers ever to have lived. He was stunningly talented in all aspects of music. One intriguing, and commonly believed, idea about Mozart's works is that they all were written quickly, easily, and in their final form. That is, they were first—and simultaneously final—drafts.

According to the romantic mythology, Mozart didn't compose music, "he simply took dictation from god."

Is it actually true that Mozart's masterpieces are first drafts? It's a little disappointing to burst such a magical idea, but no, his masterpieces are not first drafts.

Ulrich Konrad is a German scholar who has devoted years to understanding Mozart, reading every letter, public announcement, and scrap of evidence to learn Mozart's true composition process. Through his investigation, Konrad concluded that Mozart neither took dictation from god nor produced masterpiece first drafts.

Quite to the contrary, Mozart followed a conscious, persistent process, laying out the structure first, then methodically revising, moving through multiple, intensively edited drafts before reaching the works' final forms. The death of such a magical story is sad. The reality it leaves behind, however, should be at least a little comforting when you're daunted by a writing assignment. Everyone—from legendary literary authors to children—produces first drafts that must be improved with effort.

The famous book by Strunk and White states, "Remember, it is no sign of weakness or defeat that your manuscript ends up in need of major surgery. This is a common occurrence in all writing, and among the best writers."

You might think that while you're writing a paper—given the time pressure you're under—it's not the right time to work on improving. But you'd be wrong. Writing is a process as much as a means to generating a product. As such, there is no better time to improve your writing than when you are immersed in it.

Fortunately, there are many excellent guidebooks, style books, and grammar books. Don't be overwhelmed; start with just one or two. We suggest that you start with one or both of these:

The Elements of Style *by William Strunk and E.B. White*

First written in 1918, this 128-page classic is an audacious marvel of wisdom and advice. (There is a reason more than ten million copies have been sold.) Here is a taste of its wisdom: "Instead of announcing what you are about to tell is interesting, make it so."

The acclaimed writer Dorothy Parker wrote, "If you have any young friends who aspire to become writers, the second-greatest favor you can do them is to present them with copies of *The Elements of Style*. The first-greatest, of course, is to shoot them now, while they're happy."

(We'd be remiss in not also acknowledging a significant chorus of writers and teachers who love to hate on Strunk and White. This is largely in response to the book's set in stone commands. So don't worry if you feel the need to violate some of those commands.)

The Sense of Style *by Steven Pinker*

You probably wouldn't have imagined that you could be so entertained while becoming a more effective and graceful writer. Pinker argues—masterfully—that style can make the world a better place. We have no doubt that it can elevate every single thing you write.

Here are a couple of samples: "a crisp sentence, an arresting metaphor, a witty aside, an elegant turn of phrase are among life's greatest pleasures." And, "The reasons to strive for good style: to enhance the spread of ideas, to exemplify attention to detail, and to add to the beauty of the world." Admit it: that's a beautiful sentence.

Try not to get overwhelmed by the challenge of improving your writing. There are no tricks, so work with the simple, manageable goal of always improving. It may help if you wait until the revision phase of your writing to make it a focus of your efforts.

The discussion of revisions brings us to an inescapable reality (but one that is about as surprising and welcome as your dentist telling you to floss more). The thing that separates effective, interesting writing from tedious, uninspired writing is the amount of thought and effort put into it during the *revision* phase.

One of the most common mistakes is to wait until the last minute to complete a writing assignment and then turn in your first full draft. That same C+ first draft can easily become an A if you finish it just a few days early and return to the writing after a break.

Know this: when it comes to revising, your most valuable improvements will come during the revisions you make *after* you (previously) would have thought you were done. At this point, you've already put your ideas in writing and you've had a chance to sequence things appropriately and polish your delivery a bit.

3. Successful Writing Is Fun to Read
Here are some opening lines from college essays:

"I have old hands."

"Do you have body bags? The leak-proof kind . . . we need as many as you can spare!"

"I had never seen anyone get so excited about mitochondria."

The overwhelming response from the people who read a lot of essays is that the writing is boring. Remember that one or more human beings are reading your writing, and they are probably reading the work of many students.

The three lines above come from searching for 'best opening lines to a college essay.' Looking for the 'worst opening lines' reveals some of the following:

"Benjamin Franklin once said . . ."

"For each of the past three summers, I have volunteered at a summer camp for children."

It's hard to describe exactly what makes writing terrible—or simply bland and ineffective. There are just so many ways. Still, you will have a better outcome with your writing if you consider the perspective of the reader. Make their life more interesting. Put a smile on their face.

Key Aspects of Good Writing

We'll close this chapter with some advice that can improve almost any piece of writing.

- *Less is more.* One guideline for strong academic writing is to say everything relevant in as few words as possible. As you edit, search for redundancies. Look for unnecessary words and sentences. Remove them.
- *Vary sentence structure.* Here's a little tactic we like to use. Open a spreadsheet and, for some or all of your paper, enter the number of words in each of your sentences. Then calculate your average sentence length and the standard deviation.

   Now revise that section of text and craft some shorter sentences while also including the occasional longer sentence. In doing so, you'll be increasing the standard deviation of your sentence length. You'll likely also increase their readability while reducing monotony. It works.

- *Minimize monotony.* Have you included a rhetorical question now and then?
- *Preempt your critics.* A powerful way to strengthen your papers—or presentations—is to anticipate objections or criticisms of your arguments and refute them. In doing this you demonstrate not just the depth of your analysis, but also your ability to see things from another's perspective and to recognize and address common misconceptions.
- *Start strong.* It can be difficult to begin writing a paper. Consequently, in revision, your opening may need more attention than other parts. Don't skimp.

  As in real life, first impressions matter. Your first sentences can hook your reader with a provocative idea, a counterintuitive proposal, an unexpected relevance beyond the specific topic, or a funny insight.

  A longtime writing teacher at a top college (who requested anonymity), put it this way, "If the first page is well written, the instructor starts thinking of the paper as an A. If the rest isn't as good, the paper still earns a good grade because it started as an A."

  And please don't always rely on someone else's words, opening with a quotation of some sort.
- *Find your voice.* Often, college students write as if they have been issued a dictum requiring a tone that is complex, formal, dry, and boring. Somehow, while trying to sound smart, they lose their voice.

Your writing can benefit from conveying not just facts and ideas, correctly structured grammatically and punctuated, but also a bit of you. Your personality, your way of viewing the world, and your style can and should find a way into your writing. Using the suggestions above can help you find your voice, and bring life to your writing. Give it a try.

Take Home Messages

1. Perform the necessary detective work to learn your instructor's idiosyncrasies. Study the rules on grading and develop a strategy to work efficiently across your courses.

2. Effort is rarely listed on the formal syllabus. Because your instructors are human, however, they usually will value sincere demonstrations of caring and effort.

3. Use a methodical, comprehensive approach as you research, organize, and develop your narrative structure, and write a paper.

4. Make your writing fun. Think about the reader's life.

5. Even the best first draft can be improved significantly with revision. Complete a full draft early enough to take a break for at least a day and then revise. Try to take comfort in the knowledge that first drafts are hard for most people. Editing, fortunately, is fun and (relatively) easy.

HOW TO STUDY A LANGUAGE

Maybe your college requires a year or two of language study to graduate. Maybe you speak Spanish or Mandarin at home and you want a fun and easy class. Or maybe you want to turn your talent for fansubbing anime into a career. Whatever the case, chances are you'll take a language during college. Unfortunately, few students know how to study a language at the college level. Some even resent the language requirement—a feeling that often has to do with fear of something nasty called "grammar."

This chapter explains how to make the most of your language class, whether you're there by choice, or not so much. This chapter is very specific to language acquisition. Feel free to skip to the next chapter if this is not relevant to you.

If you've ever waited in line for coffee, you've had conversations that sound like this:

Barista:	How can I help you today?
You:	Small Americano.
Barista:	D'you need room?
You:	Yeah.
Barista:	Anything else I can get for you?
You:	I'm good.
Barista:	Name for the order?
You:	Casey.
Barista:	Thank you, Casey.
You:	Thanks so much.

Imagine how puzzling this conversation might sound to someone learning English. "Small Americano" is a drink, not a short U.S. citizen. "Needing room" has nothing to do with how crowded the place is; it means "wanting less coffee than the cup will hold in order to leave space for cream." "I'm good" is a strange way to say "no." "For the order," like "today" in the first line, is just filler. And the response to "thank you" in American English in this context is usually some other version of "thank you," not the textbook answer "you're welcome."

What makes this conversation hard for outsiders to understand, and even harder to participate in, is that it's based on a shared code for communicating specific information as efficiently as possible. Given what both parties want to accomplish, their use of language is actually quite straightforward. But an ESL student seeing the conversation on video is still going to be confused. To crack the code, she needs to know what specific words and phrases—Americano, room, I'm good—actually mean *here*. What won't help much is grammar.

"How many languages do you know?" The person with the most impressive answer seems to have been a nineteenth-century Italian priest named Mezzofanti, who reportedly was comfortable in more than thirty, from Hebrew to Algonquin. Going through Mezzofanti's papers in search of his secret to successful language learning, the writer Michael Erard made an unexpected discovery (spoiler alert!):

> There was one final box, what the inventario labeled as "miscellaneous." After days of looking at files and flat pages, I was surprised to see, when I opened the lid, squarish lumps. My heart jumped. I took out a lump. It was a block of paper, about three inches long and one inch wide on each side, wrapped in dry paper and tied

with red waxed string . . . On each slip of paper was written a word with a corresponding word in a different language on the reverse.

This was Mezzofanti's secret: flash cards. Erard discovered another secret, too. People who reach proficiency in many languages rarely are motivated by a practical goal, such as using Korean for business. Rather, they're people who enjoy the feeling of how their brain changes in response to repetitive tasks such as studying flash cards. The fluency in Korean, or whatever, just kind of happens at some point.

The reason is that your brain changes its structure when you learn something new. Historically, scientists identified Broca's area in the brain's left hemisphere as the primary area that helps us produce language, and Wernicke's area as the chief area for understanding language. More recently, however, neuroscientists have documented much more widespread brain involvement in language, including physical brain growth in response to language acquisition. Getting stronger physically requires muscle growth; learning a new language requires brain growth.

So, study your flash cards in the same way as you might practice a piece of music, rehearse a play, or do more reps at the gym. Yes, the goal matters, but the practice should be rewarding, too. People who can focus on their flash cards without distractions (no texting!) can even go into a sort of meditative state, similar to being immersed in a really good video game. One important difference: every second that passes with your flash cards is helping you ace the next Korean exam.

To get the most out of your flash cards, use a process that keeps track of your answers and brings back more frequently the items you're having trouble with. Start with recognition. Look at the Korean words first, then guess the English. Then flip it around so that you're looking at English and coming up with the Korean yourself.

Adding sound and pictures can help jog your memory. And embrace mnemonics, the more absurd the better. To memorize *afedersiniz*, which means "excuse me" in Turkish, Alicia imagined tennis star Roger Federer walking down the street in Istanbul bumping into people and saying "Excuse me!" Although Alicia's trip to Turkey happened more than ten years ago (and she hasn't used the language since), she still remembers the word.

The *Tao Te Ching* states, "The Tao that can be told is not the eternal Tao." Paradoxically, the biggest secret to learning new words is not to study words.

Instead of words, study phrases. Imagine our ESL student trying to learn the word "set." The *Oxford English Dictionary* gives forty-seven different meanings, and that's just for the noun. What should the student put on the back of her flash cards?

The trick is not to put the word "set" by itself anywhere. Instead, devote flash cards to phrases: "all set," "set of rules," "game, set, and match." Each of these has a precise equivalent in other languages, and it's those equivalents the student should be studying, not the slippery word "set," which in effect means nothing all by itself.

If you're studying Spanish, don't put *partido* on one side of a card and game on the other. "Game" has many meanings, including some that should be translated using *juego*, not *partido*. So make one card that says soccer game/*partido de fútbol*, and another that says zero-sum game/*juego de suma cero*. Study this way and you'll be producing phrases, not words—just like a native speaker.

———————

Look for the how.

You have studied your flash cards and you are thinking in phrases. But what about the time you spend in class? A good language class focuses on *using* the language, not talking about it. Unfortunately, many students fail to make the best use of this scheduled rehearsal time. Here are some tips for getting it right.

Typically, when we process language, what we retain is the meaning, as opposed to the specific words. And recognizing a word or phrase when someone else says it doesn't mean you can produce it. This is why you can understand every single word Martin Luther King Jr. says in his "I Have a Dream" speech, but if asked to improvise a talk on the subject of civil rights for an audience of 250,000, you probably couldn't come up with it all by yourself.

It is the same with this week's dialogue for your Mandarin class: you can reread it ten times and still freeze up when you are called on to improvise a speech about yourself. It's that critical distinction between *recognition* and *mastery* that we discuss in chapter 7; you're familiar with the dialogue, but you haven't understood it. You know "what" is being said—Bai Ying'ai is inviting Wang Peng to dinner—but not "how" to say it.

To learn the how, look at the actual words used to convey what is happening. For example, when Bai Ying'ai says that tomorrow is her friend's birthday, the word for "is" is *shì*. But when Wang Peng says he's busy today, he uses a different word for "is": *hěn*. So it seems we have two ways to say "is" in Mandarin: one is used for equivalence (A is the same as B) and the other for describing things (A has the quality of being B).

First, test this hypothesis out on other "is" sentences from your textbook to see if it's true. Then make up a few of your own sentences (the sillier the better), taking care to use the right word for "is." If you're not sure which word to use in one of your made-up sentences, ask your teacher after class. (Language teachers love questions like this.)

When you create your flash cards, don't use "is" or *shì* or *hěn* by themselves anywhere. Instead, put the whole phrase there: "Tomorrow is my birthday" and "Wang Peng is busy." If the sentences are the ones you made up, the chances are even better that you'll remember them. As with mnemonics, silly tends to be stickier in your brain. Later, when your teacher asks you to improvise a dialogue with your partner, you'll already have some of your own phrases ready to go.

OK, you've aced your dialogue. But what about the other ninety-five percent of class time—the time when other people are talking? The natural tendency is to tune out. After all, the other students are probably making mistakes, so why listen to them? Actually, you should listen. To learn why, meet Kristen.

Kristen grew up speaking one language: English. Today, she speaks four Arabic dialects, two of them so well that she's hard to distinguish from a native speaker. What's her secret? Although she's now a professor of Arabic, she was never that student sitting in the front row with her hand always raised.

In fact, Kristen was painfully shy and never spoke a word through four years of undergraduate language classes. Then, during a study abroad program in Cairo, she suddenly began speaking—almost as well as she does today. It turns out that for four years she was simply listening—but with a twist. "I was listening to my classmates," she says, "and correcting them in my head."

If you have a good language instructor, you won't get away with sitting quietly for an entire class, much less a whole year (or four). But you can still do what Kristen did and take advantage of those minutes when others are talking.

While we're on the subject of your classmates, let's clear up a complaint that college language teachers hear all the time: "The other students in my class already speak the language." Well, yes and no. It's true that your elementary Hebrew class might be full of students who went to Hebrew school for years, and the guy next to you in Russian class might speak the language with his parents at home.

However, the Hebrew school students may never have seen a news site in Hebrew, and your Russian-speaking classmate may not even know the alphabet. The reality is that the variety of language taught in college classrooms is different than the varieties people are exposed to through their families and religious communities.

It's true that so-called heritage learners can sound good enough to be intimidating—especially during the first week. But when it comes to skills like reading and writing, they often fare worse than their flash-carding, active-listening classmates. So, if you find yourself sitting next to a Chinese speaker in your Mandarin class, don't worry. Chances are she's speaking Cantonese, not Mandarin, and she's no better with character recognition than you are. Whatever the case, listen to her, and correct her in your head.

The flip side of this advice is, if you're the heritage speaker, don't imagine that you have a free ride to an easy A. Yes, you start with an advantage, but seriously, it won't last more than two or three weeks. Then you'll need to hit the textbook and the course website just like everybody else. If you don't, the Kristen sitting next to you will outperform you on the final.

———————

Now that you've learned how to read, listen, and speak effectively, let's address the last of the four old-school language skills: writing. The single biggest mistake students make when writing compositions is . . . writing compositions. That is, they make up something, perhaps because they think writing should be creative. Then they translate that made-up something into the foreign language, often word for word. The result is painful to your instructor and, worse yet, not helpful to you in learning the language.

Suppose your assignment is to write about what you did over the weekend. The first thought that pops into your head might be "I went to a football game." Should you take the sentence "Over the weekend, I went to a football game" and translate it into French or German or whatever? Probably not—for a whole stack of good reasons.

For starters, you're likely to waste many minutes wrestling with how to say "over" when it means "during." You're also likely to miss the fact that "going to" a place in many languages doesn't necessarily mean that you stayed there. And of course then there's "game," which, as we saw previously, is a can of worms all by itself.

What should you do instead? Don't lose sight of the key point: there was a sporting event. Now focus your efforts on the challenge of how you talk about sporting events in, say, French. Start with a search for "French soccer teams."

Many of the results are place names, so take one that has another part: "AS Monaco," for example. Then search for *AS Monaco nouvelles* (*nouvelles* means "news"). Thousands of articles come up—and many are impenetrably difficult—but one has a nice easy beginning: *Enfin une bonne nouvelle pour l'AS Monaco.* "Finally, some good news for AS Monaco." Now you've got a way into your essay.

If over the weekend you saw UCLA beat USC, change the sentence to *Enfin une bonne nouvelle pour l'UCLA* and now you have an opening sentence. The problem that "news" can be singular in French has been solved for you, along with a host of other grammar issues that might have tripped you up.

But (you might ask) what happened to the "I" in "Over the weekend, I . . ."? Well, it's gone, and that's good. French speakers don't usually put themselves front and center in their compositions in the same way Americans do. The more you sound like them, the more convincing you'll be as a French writer. Sometimes you're learning things and you don't even know it.

Is this plagiarism? No, because you're not trying to pass off someone else's idea as your own; you're borrowing the *how*. And that is central to what language learning is. Plus, you're not simply copying the text, you're modifying it to express what you want to say (or something close to it—which is another thing language learning is about).

Consistent with what we know about learning, this technique works best if you force yourself to retype the phrase instead of copying and pasting it. And when you add *une bonne nouvelle pour* /'some good news for' to your flash card deck, you can feel confident that you've mastered another lesson.

Take Home Messages

1. Study vocabulary first. Study phrases, not words. Use flash cards.

2. Learn to look for the how—the actual words people use to convey what is happening.

3. When others are speaking, correct them in your head.

4. Don't be intimidated by heritage speakers. If you are a heritage speaker, do not be complacent.

5. Find and emulate phrases that you find from native speakers. Modify to suit your situation.

OVERCOMING BARRIERS TO SUCCESS

RESILIENCE

Everyone Falls; Only Some Get Back Up

Knowing something is a bad idea doesn't always stop you from doing it. Linda was a student in Jay's genetics class at UCLA. Her boyfriend was in the class, too, but he was struggling. Fearful that he would not pass the class, he asked Linda to help him cheat.

If Linda would just sign his name rather than hers to the weekly quizzes, her boyfriend could accumulate sufficient points to pass. Her strong performance on the exams would be enough to get her through without the quiz points. Reluctantly, she agreed. And it worked for a few weeks. But even in a big class, other students or teaching assistants eventually can sense when something's not quite right . . . which they did. Following an investigation and hearing, the dean expelled Linda from UCLA.

By any measure of "college success," Linda had pretty much the biggest failure possible. But even still, it's possible to bounce back. You can always learn from your mistakes and, if you incorporate that knowledge into your future behavior and decision-making, it's even possible to get better outcomes.

Forced to move out of the dorm and back home, Linda had a lot of time to contemplate her mistake and the poor choices she had made. She also spent time grieving the fact that her dream of becoming a pharmacist was probably dead.

A couple of months later, however, Jay got a glimpse of the resiliency that would turn Linda's life around in a note she sent:

> *Even with good grades, it is hard to get into pharmacy school. I am worried that schools will compare me (unfavorably) with a student having the same grades but not having a dismissal on their transcript. But what can I do but give it my all? I'm glad that it's a new year. I feel that I can start off anew again.*
>
> *I'm going to start at a community college next week. I am also looking into better schools for transferring. (I doubt I'll get accepted but it's better to try than not to.) I filled out an application at the Boys and Girls club and will be volunteering there soon. That should be a lot of fun, too.*
>
> *My plan is to show that I am hardworking, committed to my studies, and able to think creatively. It's also to show them that I can learn from my mistakes.*

Contrary to assumptions we may hold about rigid admissions committees wanting only students with unblemished records, the following year Linda was accepted for transfer to USC. And eventually she gained admittance to pharmacy school, where she excelled.

Today Linda is a successful pharmacist, running her own practice. Her pathway took longer and certainly didn't follow the route that she had planned. But we think Linda would agree that she is better and wiser now than if she hadn't made these errors of judgment long ago, learned from them, and worked so hard to become the person she wanted to be.

College today presents unlimited opportunities for stress, anxiety, and failure. In a recent survey, more than half of college students reported that they had "felt overwhelming anxiety" at some point in the previous year. Stresses are common during significant life changes, and the transition to college is one of the biggest. Today, pervasive technology can magnify those potentially harmful feelings.

Technology surrounds us with images that are captivating, but many that are also deceiving and hurtful. Consider the photo-editing feature called "noise reduction." It's a tool for improving digital images by removing artifacts that interfere with the light sensor's ability to capture the photo.

It turns out, though, that in the process of removing noise, this magical tool also happens to erase wrinkles (and years) from any picture of a face. Jay likes to play with this and reports, "The further I move a little slider, the more of the 'noise' of aging in my face that I remove." Jay now is reluctant to show a photo in which he hasn't done at least a little noise reduction. Most of us prefer that younger version of ourselves; that's the version Jay would rather present to the world.

But Jay's "noise reduction" isn't the only reason why the online world looks to most people a bit better than reality. Besides improving images, people are selective about the version of their life they present to the world and this can lead to an unfortunate situation. We see only the better-looking, curated version of everyone else's lives, but we live our own life in person and unedited, reminded daily of the realities of wrinkles, missteps, struggles, and other "noise."

It's hard *not* to imagine that everyone else is skating through a trouble-free world with only victories and double rainbows, while you're nagged by anxiety and uncertainty. Another day, another photo of your friend Burt's award-winning ribs, another video verifying Mia's impeccable form at the gym, and yet another reminder of Aliyah's nonstop adventure travel (always with perfect hair). Imposter syndrome? How could we *not* feel that?

The anxiety we feel has physiological roots. Your brain is built to compare your life to the ones that you see, and it punishes you by withholding dopamine for failures to keep up with those around you. For college students, the wallop of everyone else's flawless, publicly observable life comes at a tough time. As we transition to a new phase in life and have little experience with our new circumstances, we may believe that we are alone in our failures.

The stress is exacerbated, too, by the fact that most students move away from their hometown and the close, supportive relationships they enjoyed there. On top of this, students are graduating with more long-term financial debt than previously. Plain and simple, we face many challenges as we transition to college. Resilience is necessary if we are to rise to these challenges.

What Is Resilience?

Arianne's response to being passed over as a columnist for her college's newspaper may strike you as extreme: "Right now this failure seems to be the major catastrophe of my existence on earth. My life is in shambles."

More perplexingly still, Arianne was a Harvard student at this emotional low point in her life. When a Harvard student feels totally defeated by a minor setback, it is akin to a child being devastated because their beautiful new scooter is the wrong shade of blue. And it's no consolation if a parent says, "you should be happy; most children in the world don't even get scooters." Such statements have zero impact on the child's misery in the face of plenty.

How is it possible to feel terrible when things are going well overall, in an objective sense? The answer is that our brains are exquisitely sensitive to changes in our situation. Using tiny sensors, researchers have shown that people have big emotional responses to seemingly trivial events. Specifically, the participants played an investment game for a few dollars. Even small wins resulted in dopamine flooding the brain, while the tiniest of setbacks created a dopamine drought.

Arianne felt her life was "in shambles" after her minor setback because her brain was bereft of dopamine at that moment. Increased dopamine—and the happiness it generates—requires both having an outcome better than expected *and* better than other people. At the molecular level, we are built to be sensitive and envious.

Fortunately, this makes resiliency possible. Our emotional response to failure—and to minor setbacks, too—is extreme but temporary. To succeed, we must persist. We will feel better and we can recover.

Indeed, Arianne's setback was temporary. Her full name is Arianne Cohen, and she now has an amazing writing career. Among her many successes, she writes for the *NY Times*, *Fast Company*, *Bloomberg Businessweek*, and even *Popular Mechanics*. Martha Stewart devoted an entire show to Arianne Cohen—a rare honor.

Arianne became successful not by being perfect, but rather by investigating her weaknesses. She says, for example, "flaunt your flaws," and give yourself a reality check to determine if "you're seeing yourself as the world sees you."

Maybe like Arianne after her early failure, you are acquainted with the feeling that your 'entire life' is in shambles? When it comes to resilience, the nature and magnitude of the challenges we encounter are not particularly relevant. Much more important is how we respond to our struggles and perceived failures.

When struggling with something—learning the material for a class, perhaps, or working to improve a relationship, or trying to land an important internship—a person may embrace the challenge. Or they may give up. Resilience is the ability to recover and thrive in the face of failure, struggles, and disappointment.

Resilience is not, however, a trait that is either present or absent in someone. Rather, we can manifest it (or not) in varying degrees, depending on the situation. Most importantly, resiliency is a personality trait that you can cultivate.

Our goal in this chapter is more ambitious than simply teaching the skill of coping with failure. Rather it is to provide tools to bounce back from failure in a way that enables better outcomes than would have been possible without failure.

Hilda Solis's high school guidance counselor described her as "not college material" and encouraged her to become a secretary instead. Pushing past this "guidance," she became the first in her family to attend college (and graduate school). After later getting elected to the U.S. House of Representatives, Hilda Solis actually did become a secretary: the U.S. Secretary of Labor. She was the first Hispanic to ever serve in this position.

In his first auditions, Sidney Poitier wasn't simply rejected. He was mocked and urged to quit acting and get a job as a dishwasher. Dedicating himself to his profession, however, Poitier became hugely successful, winning the Academy Award for Best Actor, and receiving the highest civilian honor in the United States, the Presidential Medal of Freedom.

Stories of failure and recovery reveal some of the most endur-ing and important lessons in life. That's why, beyond simply repeating these stories, it is important to extract from them practical lessons for success. Let's begin with Michael Jordan, who was famously cut from his high school basketball team only to rebound to a level of fame that extended far beyond his basketball achievements. For some time, Jordan was the most recognized person on the planet.

Here are Michael Jordan's thoughts on failure:

> *I've missed more than 9,000 shots in my career. I've lost almost 300 games. Twenty-six times, I've been trusted to take the game-winning shot and missed. I've failed over and over and over again in my life. And that is why I succeed.*

Hearing the failure stories of megastars, it is easy to dismiss them. Michael Jordan was so talented that he obviously was going to succeed. "I can't learn anything from Michael Jordan because I don't have world-class skills." But the notion that talent ensures success is wrong. In fact, Michael Jordan created his victories from work and competitiveness. He did not roll out of bed and collect six NBA championships with natural talent alone.

Ron Coley, one of Jordan's high school coaches said, "I met him in tryouts, but there was nothing particularly outstanding in tryouts. He did not make the varsity team as a sophomore." After not making the team, Jordan states, "When I got home and I told my mother I was cut, I was demoralized; I didn't want to play any more sports. I felt like the coach didn't like me."

Jordan's mother told him to work harder, and the subsequent year Jordan made varsity after a summer where he did just that. "He focused. He would practice all day. That basketball never left his hand." This productive response to failure (with an assist to mom) was the first step to success.

In the NBA draft, Michael Jordan was picked third, which means that he was not even considered the best among the players leaving college in that year. Looking back, it seems obvious that talent made Michael Jordan the best. Being drafted third and not making varsity on his high school team until his junior year, however, contributed significantly to his success, as both these incidents motivated Jordan to work harder.

One more story before we move on. Here is a list of Abraham Lincoln's early "achievements": lost job, defeated for state legislature, failed in business, had nervous breakdown, defeated for Speaker, defeated for nomination for Congress, defeated for U.S. Senate, defeated for nomination for vice president, again defeated for U.S. Senate.

After a quarter century of struggle and setback, however, Abraham Lincoln became president and then wrote both the Gettysburg Address and the Emancipation Proclamation. No one's life is over until they quit. Even decades of defeat do not mean that you cannot excel. Never give up.

Failure Happens to Everyone. It Doesn't Reveal Some Unchangeable Aspect of Who We Are.

Academic failure isn't a competition, but if it were, George Church would make the Hall of Fame. Contributing to a collection of stories called *Reflections on Rejections*, Church noted that his failures began when he was required to repeat the ninth grade. Later, Church was accepted to graduate school at Duke. However, he flunked out of the program. He held onto his dismissal letter as a motivating reminder:

Examination of your record for the past semester reveals that you earned a grade of F in a course in your major field. Earning a grade of F in the major field occasions withdrawal from a degree program. Consequently, you are no longer a candidate for the Doctor of Philosophy degree. We regret that this action is necessary and hope that whatever problems . . . may have contributed to your lack of success . . . at Duke will not keep you from successful pursuit of a productive career.

These failures helped George Church change his habits and re-focus his approach to education. He has managed a spectacular rebound. As a professor of genetics at Harvard Medical School and MIT, George Church has coauthored 622 research papers and been awarded 156 patents, as of 2021. *Newsweek* featured him in an article called "Ten Hottest Nerds," and, in 2017, he was selected as one of *Time Magazine's* 100 Most Influential People. How do you like him now, Duke?

It's easy to forget that failure is inextricably linked to success. This is truer now than ever before, given the heavily edited, picture-perfect social media world that seems to want to crush our spirit some days. More specifically, it is essential to under-stand that failure doesn't necessarily carry special information about your ultimate ability to achieve success in an endeavor. Failure never means: "You cannot ever do this. So, give up."

But we are vulnerable to such thoughts. Whether you realize it or not, you go through your life with some theories about cause and effect relationships in the world. When it comes to intellectual capabilities, for example, you might believe that they are just something that a person is born with. If you lack a natural aptitude for something, you may believe that's just unlucky for you. As it turns out, however, not only is this theory not accurate, just believing it has some pretty terrible consequences.

In a large study of high school students, half of the students learned about the achievements of Marie Curie, Albert Einstein, and other scientists as part of their curriculum. The other half learned not only about the scientists' achievements, but also about their personal and intellectual struggles. This seemingly minor difference in the curricula was associated with two very big differences in students' lives:

1) Those who learned only about great scientific achievements were more likely to attribute them to the scientists' natural abilities—talents which distinguished them from everyone else.

2) Those students who learned about the science stars' personal struggles actually learned more science *and* got higher grades!

Simply becoming aware that smart, famous, successful people have failed actually helps you to learn more and perform better. In related research, students having a "growth mindset"—the understanding that intellectual abilities are something that you develop and that can improve—had significantly better performance in classes and were more likely to complete the courses they took. With the right mindset, you can bounce back better and achieve much more.

You Can Learn Important Things from Failure (That You Can't Learn from Success)

Getting an F in college is considered bad. In other settings, however, earning the equivalent of an F is central to the learning process. For example, the path to mastery of nearly every video game requires extensive and repeated failure. As Charlie, aged ten, explains, "That's how you learn what to do." Through those failures comes learning and, ultimately, success. (You can now tell your parents that playing video games is helping improve your resilience. You're welcome.)

Similarly, pilots training in simulators encounter challenges that are designed to create failure. This effectively guides them toward greater mastery of their profession, while building their resilience. In military training, too, soldiers are made to experience challenges *designed* to result in failure! William Blake wrote, "The road of excess leads to the palace of wisdom . . . You never know what is enough unless you know what is more than enough."

Our academic world is a messed-up outlier when it comes to embracing failure. From video games to military and pilot training, effective teaching relies on the value of exploring—and failing—in novel situations. Failure is an essential aspect of learning.

The potential lessons from failure aren't restricted to better equipping you to solve a problem or meet a challenge. As the inventor of Post-it notes discovered, sometimes failure helps you to see that you were working on the wrong problem.

Aiming to develop a high-strength adhesive, Dr. Spencer Silver seemed to fail when he produced only a low-strength (though reusable) adhesive. That turned out to be a beautiful solution, just to a different problem. Today, those not-very-sticky slips of paper generate more than one billion dollars in revenue each year.

Further complicating matters, some failures have nothing at all to do with your efforts or abilities. There may be factors beyond your control. Toward the end of graduate school, Jay applied to the National Science Foundation for its prestigious Dissertation Improvement Grant. Jay's proposal wasn't merely rejected; in the scathing reviews it was completely crushed.

During the subsequent year, Jay had a new PhD advisor who asked why he wasn't applying for the Dissertation Improvement Grant. In response, Jay recounted his sob story about the previous year's smackdown. The experienced professor laughed off the failure. Grant application success or failure, he said, is not always related to the quality of a project. "It's like a lottery—but you've got to buy a ticket."

The advisor suggested that Jay submit the *same* proposal with no revisions in response to the previous year's criticisms. Imagine Jay's surprise when he was selected to receive the grant. Of course, just as Jay no longer needed to feel demoralized by the original rejection, neither should he take credit for the praise heaped on him when his coal nugget of a proposal was rechristened as a diamond.

You Can Become More Resilient. Here's How.

Here's a useful rule of thumb that applies to just about any endeavor.

> *As long as you use the same methods as in the past, you are likely to get the same outcome.*

This is fine if everything is going swimmingly. But if you've just experienced a disappointing result—a botched interview, maybe, or a bombed exam—then you probably need to make some changes.

For failure to be more than just a bummer, revisit and examine it. Contemplate its potential causes. Find kernels of value. Deconstruct the failure. In doing that, you reduce your likelihood of future failures and your life gets better.

Believe it or not, an important first step is to explore your emotions. In the *Journal of Behavioral Decision Making*, researchers described experimental results with serious practical value. People who contemplated their emotions—particularly their bad feelings associated with a failure—were better able to correct their mistakes in subsequent efforts.

Next—even though the prospect might make you cringe—turn your failures into stories. Celebrate your less-than-stellar moments as you discuss and dissect them. Rather than apologizing or distancing yourself from the failures, find the comedy. Use it to help you bounce back and navigate your way toward recovery.

In normalizing our failures, storytelling carries enormous value. It is cathartic, but it's also a powerful tool for illuminating imperfect moments in ways that enable you to visualize constructive alternative pathways for next time.

Addressing your own pain can even improve your health. One scientific study asked people who were HIV-positive to write about their feelings. Patients who were more expressive in exploring their emotional response to their condition were healthier. Expressing your emotions, particularly your bad feelings, can make you healthier and live longer. Investigating and discussing how you feel is a key step to recovery.

Want more evidence? Track down the video series *"Stanford, I screwed up."* In one video, for example, Julie Haims describes getting a D in communications in her first semester at Stanford. She explains that getting a low grade in a class that was supposed to be easy meant to her, at that time, that she was not fit for Stanford. For Julie, all aspects of the course were overwhelming. She was too embarrassed to even talk about her performance, and began crying when, months later, she finally discussed the grade with her parents.

For Julie, the resilient road to success—in the form of graduating from Stanford and venturing beyond—included seeking help. "It was nerve-racking as hell to go to somebody and say, 'Hi . . . I have been doing very poorly in this class, and I think I need some help.'"

Seeing others share their stories of failure and resilience will make you smile. Who knew that so many smarties had a D– or F or C– lurking on their transcripts? Continue watching and their stories of bouncing back begin to inspire you.

One productive way to learn from a failure can be in the form of a "Failure Deconstruction." For one of your failures, try to figure out and articulate the answers to these questions:

1. What was the desired outcome you wanted? In retrospect, was it reasonable?
2. What exactly was the nature of your failure?
3. Did you seek help? Did you take the advice that was given?
4. At what point did you identify that you were in trouble? Could you have seen it coming sooner? How?
5. Had you structured things so that you could get feedback about whether you were on track? If not, why not?
6. What changes did you make in response to the feedback you got?

Record your answers in a "Failure Notebook." You can be flexible in interpreting these questions. Evaluating a failing romantic relationship, for example, requires a slightly different approach than a failing performance in a college class.

You can't shy away from confronting yourself with the hard questions. And the more significant you perceive the failure to be, the more detail and time you should devote to your deconstruction.

The range of possible explanations for your failures may be wider than you imagine. Have you considered the possibility that you failed because you were doing the wrong thing? Maybe that's the message. The solution isn't always some version of "Try harder. Be smarter." Sometimes it's closer to "Know thyself." Are pre-law studies about your dreams or your family's dreams for you? Or are they about the aspirations of the ten-year-old version of you?

Follow-up your Failure Deconstruction with your Recovery Construction. Use your answers to the Failure Deconstruction to develop a recovery plan. Can you fix this failure? If not, how can you reduce the likelihood that you have another failure for similar reasons? Your recovery plans will illuminate how you may need to change your behaviors:

- improving your study techniques;
- exploring and utilizing the many resources that your campus has to offer;
- learning when and how to ask for help;
- nurturing and relying on the support system your friends, family, and mentors provide;
- seeking feedback from others who are succeeding where you are struggling.

Implementing these plans—and refining them as you gain experiences—holds the key to improving your efforts and your ability to operate effectively as a student (and as a human).

Why did a pharmacy school accept Linda after she was expelled from UCLA for cheating? Kindness? Probably not. Something more universal and predictable likely explains Linda's ability to recover.

If you look up ratings of pharmacy schools, the 2020 *US News and World Report* lists the University of North Carolina at Chapel Hill as number one. The rankings of pharmacy schools are based on a wide variety of factors including alumni salaries, peer ratings, and student quality. The student quality measurement is a combination of grade point average and a standardized test score (in this case, the Pharmacy College Admission Test).

A variety of great outcomes redound to highly ranked pharmacy schools. Professors want to work at successful schools, students want to attend them, and employers want to hire their graduates. And for the people who run pharmacy schools—deans and other administrators—as their school's ranking improves, so too do their career prospects. With so much on the line, pharmacy schools compete fiercely with each other to achieve top rankings. But what does this have to do with Linda and her expulsion?

Student quality, as factored into pharmacy school rankings, does not include any data on previous expulsions. Thus, with her later good grades and high test scores, Linda was able to help her pharmacy school improve its own "grade." Of course, if the school thought Linda was going to repeat her offense, then they would not have accepted her. Fortunately, Linda pursued a course that convinced the pharmacy school that this was unlikely.

Take Home Messages

1. Failures, struggles, and disappointments range from the tiny and seemingly trivial, to the catastrophic. Furthermore, our brains are built to literally freak out in response to bad news. We encounter setbacks in academic, social, professional, and ethical situations.

2. Resilience is the ability to recover and thrive in the face of these challenges. It's a trait we all should (and can) cultivate.

3. Failure is extremely common—universal, in fact. It doesn't reflect some flaw or unchangeable aspect of you. Simply understanding that your personality, intelligence, and resilience are malleable and can improve makes you better.

4. On its own, failure is just painful and undesirable. With an eye on learning from failure, you can gain valuable insights into how to be better and progress toward better outcomes.

5. Storytelling is an important step toward banishing the inappropriate and unhelpful shame. Being expressive turns something that may be unknown and, consequently, debilitating, into a familiar and ordinary part of the process of learning to succeed.

6. You can (and must) become more resilient. Resilience requires analyzing your failures, embracing the reality that failure is part of your (and everyone's) life, and extracting value from the event—in the form of specific lessons—to improve your outcomes in the future.

EXAM POSTMORTEM

How to Learn from the Experience

On a snowy morning in Ann Arbor, Michigan, many years ago, Terry rode his bike to pick up his first midterm exam for advanced organic chemistry. He went to the professor's office and found the box with the graded exams (the world was less concerned with privacy and exams were routinely left in hallways). He rummaged through and found his exam, which had a bright red **F** on the top. He had failed the exam, earning just half the possible points.

When we get bad news like this, we get angry. Or we cry. Or both. And our first impulse is to close our eyes, put the test in a sealed drawer or a garbage can, and move on. This, of course, is precisely the wrong approach.

Despite his disastrous beginning in this class, Terry was able to recover. This was because, for the first time, he learned a fundamental truth about exam improvement and made it a central component of his processes for studying and learning. As a result, he went from that F on the first midterm to an A on the comprehensive final exam, enabling him to salvage an A– in the course. What's the secret to improving your exam performances? Read on.

In *A Scandal in Bohemia*, Sherlock Holmes says, "It is a capital mistake to theorize before one has data. Insensibly one begins to twist facts to suit theories, instead of theories to suit facts."

An exam, especially a failed exam, should be viewed like a crime scene. It is to be studied, not ignored. If you listen to it very closely, it can speak to you—in ways both specific and general. After contemplating his performance and the tough position it put him in, Terry took his F and tracked down the exam answer key posted outside the professor's office.

Step 1 in Terry's detective work was to methodically record the correct answers—not with a camera—but rather by writing them out, word for word.

Step 2 was to borrow the class notes of a particularly hard-working student, Maria. With these notes, Terry got to work. For each exam question, he used 1) Maria's notes, 2) the course syllabus, and 3) the textbook to find both the source of the question and the location of the answer.

In tracking down the source of each question and answer, Terry recognized a pattern. Every single exam question could be found somewhere in the class notes. The professor had not pulled any trick question from out of thin air. Quite on the contrary, the questions and the answers were all there in Maria's meticulous notes (and on Maria's near-perfect exam). So plainly were the exam questions and answers in the class notes, it almost seemed like the professor *wanted* students to find them.

When Terry looked through the assigned readings, he could also find the answers, but usually only after skipping around a lot, reading dozens of pages (many of which were not particularly relevant). Sometimes the pages of the textbook that contained the answers were not even in the chapters assigned for that portion of the class.

So, the exam questions and their answers could be found easily in the lecture notes. And although that information was also in the textbook, it could not be found there so easily and unambiguously. Here is another relevant fact. Because Terry's organic chemistry class was at 8:00am, he rarely made the bitterly cold trek from his dorm room to class. Instead, he diligently read and outlined the assigned chapters.

Step 3 was to use his findings to craft a new plan. Based on his detective work, Terry committed to 1) going to class every day—even when it was below zero (literally) and dark; 2) taking good notes; and 3) rewriting the class notes in his own words, before each exam.

What happened? The future exams all seemed easy. The professor told the students what to study. And then the professor asked exam questions on that material.

————————

There seems to be an obvious take home message here: "go to class and take good notes." But that's not it. The actual message is this: study the first exam of a professor to learn their *modus operandi* (M.O.), or "method of operation." Each professor has an M.O. for creating exams, and the first exam offers students a valuable chance to study the crime scene.

In this case, the professor wrote exams drawn closely from the lectures. Terry, not always a fan of attending lectures, had received an A in his previous chemistry class without attending a single lecture. That professor had created exams straight from the textbook.

Professors have diverse exam-writing styles. In order to be successful, a student should understand how each of their professors creates exams. There are clues in the syllabus. And many more clues are revealed as the professor describes the course content during class meetings. You should make sure to capture those sorts of clues in your notes—don't limit yourself to taking notes only on the content.

The best data, however, come from analysis of the actual first exam. Or better still, from exams the professor has given in previous years. A professor's exam-writing M.O. rarely changes much from year to year and course to course.

Just as professors have an M.O., so too do students. Terry had a student, Barde, who earned the lowest midterm score in a class of 500 students. Due to this poor performance, meetings were arranged for Barde with the dean and with Terry, his instructor. What did Terry tell Barde during the meeting? The short version of Terry's message was this: "You failed this exam. If you don't change your methods, you will fail again."

Because this short message is difficult for most students to absorb, Terry delivered a longer version:

> Barde, I have some bad news and some good news. The bad news is that you did very poorly on the midterm. In fact, you got one of the lowest grades in the class. But the good news is that this exam is a small part of the overall course grade. So, you can still get a good grade in the class.
>
> In order to earn a better grade, Barde, I suggest that you change the way that you approach the class, particularly how you prepare for the exams. Your grade may have been bad luck. And your

exam performance may not accurately reflect your mastery of the material. Nonetheless, you will be better off if you assume that this grade is truly what you earned and deserve.

Even more importantly, you must understand that your bad grade is a wake-up call to change. If you do not heed the wake-up call and instead prepare for the next exam in the same fashion as you did for this exam, you will almost certainly get the same bad outcome.

In this case, unfortunately, Barde did not change his behavior and ended up with a D+ in the course.

———————————

Let's get back to your exam postmortem. We've already discussed how your exam can be a valuable *general* learning experience because it helps you to understand how your professor creates exams. It can provide big value in *specific* ways, too.

Suppose you are a professor and give an exam to your class. On the exam, nearly everyone gets problem #3 wrong. Or maybe on one of the multiple-choice questions nearly everyone answers incorrectly, with everyone choosing the same wrong answer. Would this information be useful to you? Of course.

If you were the professor, you would benefit from rethinking the way you taught the material covered in problem #3. After all, it's clear that you weren't successful at teaching that material. Similarly, that multiple-choice distractor that fooled everyone? That suggests that your students still hold a common misconception. Not only do you need to clear things up, you may even need to help your students *unlearn* whatever inaccurate ideas caused them to select that particular wrong answer.

Students, too, can benefit from using data to guide their studying process. Studying previous exams closely to determine your professor's exam-writing M.O. won't help you learn about your own specific strengths and weaknesses. Your seventy percent is not the same as your classmate's seventy percent on the exam. Consequently, your best study plan for the remainder of the term is probably not the same either.

Identify exactly which topics and ideas require more of your attention. Next, identify which aspects of your study methods translated into higher performance, and which seemed less effective. To do these things, create a table of your errors, tagging each in as many ways as possible. For starters:

1. Evaluate your performance on essay questions relative to multiple choice questions. Where did you lag behind? Where did you perform relatively well? Look for patterns. Did your study method serve you well?
2. Identify common threads in your writing performances. Were you hurt by consistent weaknesses, such as in the structuring of your essays? Were you consistently imprecise in the definitions that you provided? Or did you fall short when illustrating your ideas with accurate and appropriate examples?
3. Evaluate the distribution of your errors across the different topics covered. On which topics were your scores consistently the lowest? On which did you excel? Why might that be? Did specific misconceptions interfere with your mastering of the content?

Armed with detailed information about what you know and don't know, you can be more effective at finding remedies for your deficiencies and more efficient in how you spend your study time.

Take Home Messages

1. Poor exam grades carry a message that you need to change your exam preparation techniques. Listen to the message.

2. When your exam is returned to you, evaluate the effectiveness of your specific study plan on that exam. If you performed poorly, you must change your approach to preparing for future exams in that class.

3. Every professor has a *modus operandi* for writing exams. When your exam is returned to you, using notes from the lectures, the syllabus, and the textbook, determine the source of each question and the location of its answer. From this information, develop and adhere to a study plan that will prepare you for the type of exam that your particular professor is going to write.

CAREER PLANNING

GETTING INTO THE GRADUATE SCHOOL OF YOUR CHOICE

The Process (and the Secret)

"Your transcript is literally the worst I have ever seen." A Yale professor said this when, after college, Jay visited Yale to discuss graduate schools. The professor was right. Jay had applied to graduate school with a transcript that included more than one F! Seems like a doomed mission.

It wasn't until he neared the end of his five years in college that Jay came to the realization that he wanted to go to graduate school. This desire became more concrete when he learned about a master's degree program in environmental studies at Yale that looked amazing.

But going to graduate school isn't as simple as deciding to go and finding a desirable program. Jay's grades as an undergraduate student spanned the full range, from great to terrible. He had been a slow starter, struggling for the first few years. As a consequence—at least by the critical measure of GPA—he had been a poor student.

In fact, Jay had failed several classes. (Can we please not dwell on that difficult time?–JP). But did a low GPA doom Jay's plans? No. The pathway to admittance to graduate school is less rigid than you might imagine. Fortunately, even if you find yourself in a similar position, all hope is not lost.

Skipping ahead, Jay did get into Yale for the master's degree and, two years later, a PhD program at Harvard. In this chapter, we'll explore how something like that can happen.

Understand the Process

Nearly forty percent of those with college degrees go on to earn a graduate degree. The very fact that you're reading this means it is likely you will be among these multi-degree holders one day. At some point, you may be researching graduate programs and strategizing about how to maximize your chances of getting into the best possible program for you. Advanced degrees can be divided into two groups: professional schools and graduate schools.

Professional schools train you for a specific career. These include medical and nursing school, dental school, pharmacy school, business school, law school, education schools, and many others. Professional schools confer degrees such as MD (medicine), JD (law), and MBA (business).

These professional schools accept large numbers of students from huge applicant pools. The sheer volume of applicants reduces schools' ability to delve much beyond undergraduate grades and test scores. For professional programs, the myriad guidebooks' advice is accurate: "Get good grades and high scores on the MCAT/LSAT/GMAT."

If you are sure that you are going to a professional school, our advice is to maximize your GPA and standardized test scores. If you like, you can move to chapter 17.

Graduate schools award master's or PhD degrees in fields ranging from archeology to English to economics. The time it takes to get a graduate degree varies a lot. For some master's degrees, it's just a year. Most, however, are closer to two. People take five to seven years, on average, to earn a PhD. Graduate schools are less concerned with training you for a particular job. Rather, their focus is on training you to conduct original research.

Doing your own research is very different from taking a standard undergraduate course, and so requires a different set of skills. Consequently, good undergraduate grades do not necessarily assure success in graduate school. As a result, imperfect undergraduate grades are less of a barrier for graduate school acceptance.

One fact that is not widely known, however, is that most PhD programs will not cost you a cent. Yes, you read that right! Not only will the school pay your PhD tuition, in most cases they also will offer you sufficient additional money—in the form of a stipend, grant, fellowship, or research/teaching assistantship—to live on without needing loans or extra income. You won't be rich as a PhD student, but you'll be able to make ends meet.

For the remainder of this chapter, we'll discuss the specific steps that you can take to help you get the best possible outcome if you are apply for a PhD program. But first we need to address two significant misconceptions that you may hold:

Misconception 1: Great grades and test scores are essential.

Misconception 2: Great grades and test scores are sufficient for getting accepted.

In both cases, you're wrong. In fact, the chair of one graduate admissions committee at an Ivy League school said, "Every year I receive forty applications with perfect GRE scores, and I rarely admit any of them."

Moreover, as most applicants are rejected, many candidates with great grades are not accepted. Additionally, because most PhD programs admit only a very small number of students (often a dozen or fewer each year), they can (and do) look beyond grades and test scores.

PhD programs are eager to do everything possible to find those students who will be the best fit. The better you can demonstrate that, the more likely you'll be to get one of those valuable, limited spots in the program you want. Let's explore what it means to be a "good fit" with a program.

PhD Programs: You're Not Just Looking for a School. You're Looking for a Person

Understanding the acceptance process is the key to getting admitted. This might sound obvious, but it's not. For programs leading to the PhD degree, some less obvious factors are critical. It's hard enough getting accepted when you know the criteria exactly. It's a whole lot more challenging when you're not even certain what you're supposed to do!

Here's the critical, but underappreciated, fact: you are not just looking for a school. You're also looking for an individual professor. Professors are the gatekeepers—even more so than the admissions committees. Why? To earn a PhD, along with coursework you must produce a dissertation. This is essentially a book, which describes original research that you have conducted—with or under the supervision of a faculty member—and its significance to your field of study.

Within a PhD program, you will be part of a department and you will have a primary advisor—a professor in that department—along with a thesis committee of two or three other professors. Your advisor will be the most important person in your professional life. That person, with input from the other members of your committee, will be responsible for specifying your academic program and evaluating your progress.

- Your advisor will determine which classes you will take as part of your graduate training.
- They will help you home in on exactly what it is that you would like to study.
- They will help you craft a research project through which you will learn the necessary methods to be an academic researcher. (At the extremes, in some disciplines your primary advisor will almost *tell you* the topic for your PhD research project.)
- They will help you to understand and navigate the academic world for their field. They will instruct you about books to read, conferences to attend, and ways of obtaining grants and other sources of funding for your research.
- Ultimately, they will be the person that decides when your performance is sufficient for you to graduate and receive your degree. Their mentorship will continue long after you graduate, and they typically play a significant role in helping you to find and secure a job.

Clearly, your advisor will make a significant investment of time and effort into your education and your development as a scholar. It should not come as a surprise that they play the major role in the decision as to whether you are accepted into the program in the first place.

If accepted, you will be a part of your advisor's life for many years. More often than not, your PhD advisor will be close enough to you that you will invite them to your wedding (and they will want to come). It's that sort of relationship.

Your professional successes and failures will be a reflection of your advisor and have an impact on their professional reputation.

They must want you in their life and believe that it will be a relationship that will bring benefits to them. For these reasons, you must take great care to identify and approach potential advisors as part of the process by which you complete your graduate school application.

Additionally—and nontrivially—if a potential advisor decides that they think you would be a good graduate student, and they want you in their program, their endorsement is even more important than your grade point average, test scores, or any other aspect of your application.

Finding Potential Advisors

Unlike applying for college, when applying for most PhD programs you must identify one or more faculty members who would potentially serve as your advisor in graduate school. Figuring out how to do this may be the part of the application process for which your efforts can have the greatest impact on boosting your chances of acceptance. We'll guide you through this, but prior to this step you need to complete some homework.

First, *where* would you like to go (or not go)? That's a critical step. Are there cities or parts of the country you absolutely must—or must not—live? That is not a trivial question. This is your life, and if it matters to you where you live (as it does to many people), this is the time to remind yourself that *you* are the only person in charge of your life.

Second, you also must think about the features of a school you would be interested in attending. Small versus large, public versus private, top-ranked and ultra-competitive or laid-back and maybe a bit lower on the rankings list. Reviewing published rankings can be helpful. Each ranking process has its own idiosyncrasies and biases, so don't worry too much about small distinctions among schools. The lists published by *US News and World Report* cover programs in all the major disciplines and are a good place to start. If nothing else, you'll get a nice overview of your options. It's also valuable to consult with the mentors you cultivated during college.

From these considerations, you can generate a list of schools for further exploration. Then your work becomes much more specific. From each potential school, you'll need the faculty listing for all professors in the program. Fortunately, this information is collected and organized for you by the departments and made available on their websites.

Your task is to read through each faculty member's description of their research interests. From the lists of faculty research interests, identify professors whose work you find interesting. Could you imagine working with them? Narrow this down to your top one or two professors from each school by reading some of their research publications. You don't need to read every single book or article they have written, just enough to determine whether you'd like to learn more about them. Focus on their more recent research publications.

The next steps are very labor-intensive and time-consuming. That's why, as you investigate graduate programs and potential advisors, you'll want to limit your short list. Depending on how competitive the programs are, you should identify your top five to eight schools.

Contacting Potential Advisors

With your refined list of schools and professors, you can begin to plan contacting individuals. Ideally, you should be at this stage in September, one year prior to when you intend to begin graduate school. Once you have identified someone who might be a good match as an advisor, it's time to make a connection and sell yourself.

Seek to demonstrate two attributes. First, that you will be a successful graduate student, able to conduct and complete original research. Second, that you are a person with whom others (professors and other graduate students) will want to spend time.

There is an infinite variety of ways to do this. As a rule of thumb, anticipate implementing a full strategy that entails three to five notes per professor on your list, with the later messages including substantive discussion and, ultimately, a brief in person meeting sometime near the deadline for applications.

With each successive contact of a professor, your goals will be different.

- In your first communication, your goal is to get a response that allows for subsequent correspondence. Nothing more.
- In your second and third notes, your primary goals are to convey that you are honestly interested in the research they conduct and that you have more than a cursory understanding of it. You need for them to engage with you.
- Keep in mind that, in these messages, you aim to demonstrate intelligent curiosity, combined with an appreciation for the reality that, by simply having read a couple of their publications you do not imagine that you could teach them something about their own research area. Be humble.
- If you succeed in these goals, with your next message your sole aim is to get them to agree to meet you in person.
- Assuming all goes well with these interactions, the goal of your final note will be to thank them for meeting with you, and to confirm for them that you are indeed applying to their program and hope they'll keep an eye out for your application.

Critically, with each of these contacts you must also demonstrate that you are articulate and respectful, while intriguing them sufficiently to make them wonder whether you might be the mythical Dream Graduate Student/Unicorn. That perfect graduate student is productive, no-drama, low-maintenance, creative, charismatic, interesting, mature, and solidly dependable. It's pretty much a cakewalk, right?

In your correspondence and in-person meetings, make sure to demonstrate that you've done your homework, but also to convey your excitement and enthusiasm. You are selling them on your ability to conduct research based on doable, clearly articulated, coherently conceived questions that you want to ask.

This is not the time to wax poetically about your dreams or goals. Nor is it necessarily important to explain the interesting path which took you to where you are today. Moreover, your first contact with your potential advisor doesn't need to mention anything about working specifically with them or applying for their graduate program. It is to converse about mutual research interests. Demonstrate how interesting, articulate, thoughtful, and modest you are. Hook them first. Then worry about the less-interesting-to-them issue of your application.

Getting Personal Contact and Closing the Deal

There are a variety of ways to increase your chances of getting to meet face-to-face with potential advisors. We cannot overstate the value of making this happen. You may even have to resort to something like this, near the end of your second note:

> *If your schedule permits, it would be really helpful to me if we could meet briefly. Currently, my schedule is quite flexible. And, as it turns out, I will be in Boston during the week of the 20th to*

24th of November. If you have 15 minutes to talk sometime that week, it would be easy for me to stop by. I realize that this is rather short notice. If you are not free that week, I would be happy to reschedule for a date that is convenient for you.

You should make every effort to become more than a faceless, generic application in a pile. Admissions committees make all the applications available to faculty members. This is when the prospective advisor you have contacted can indicate on your file, "I would very much like to take this student." Because there is an overabundance of qualified people, having someone specifically single you out and advocate for you can be the critical edge that tips the decision in your favor.

With your in-person meeting, the aim is to confirm what you have conveyed in your written correspondence: you are thoughtful, enthusiastic, and mature. ***You are already thinking like a graduate student.*** The professors are not trying to simply identify promising, smart young people. Their goals are pragmatic and personal. They're seeking someone to boost their own reputation and success, someone who will make their life better.

Prepare a range of informed talking points, including questions that will allow the professor to describe the projects of other graduate students working with them. If they appear willing, let them give you a tour of the offices, labs, or other spaces in which you'd be working.

Help the professor to see that you're a competent, courteous, professional student, and that you're ready to hit the ground running. When you leave this meeting, as well as in a brief follow-up thank you note, make it clear that you'll be applying to their school, that you would love the opportunity to work with them, and that you'd appreciate it if they might "look for my application when it comes through."

For Jay, the graduate school application process included visiting several Yale professors, including the one (noted previously) who said, "This is literally the worst transcript I have ever seen." That's never pleasant to hear, but it needn't be fatal to having a positive meeting.

Jay spoke with the professors about their work, much less so about himself. And he kept his conversations short. In the few cases for which it was clear the professor was enjoying the conversation, Jay let it continue. Based on these conversations, some of the professors became convinced that Jay was right for the program.

Jay believes that he might not have been accepted if he had perfect grades. "If I had great grades, I probably wouldn't have felt the need to bother with personal contact." That would have been the wrong approach. Over the years we have heard many professors say, "I would never consider taking someone as a graduate student if I hadn't spoken to them in person." And this is at schools where in-person interviews are not even an "official" part of the application process! Some of the most important rules in the world are not written down.

Jay advanced his own agenda by talking about the other person. Adam Smith famously wrote, "It is not from the benevolence of the butcher, the brewer, or the baker that we expect our dinner, but from their regard to their own interest." Similarly, Jay did not speak about how acceptance would help him. Rather, Jay focused on the professors' view of the world.

Demonstrating Follow-through:
Your Application and Personal Statement

Graduate school applications require you to include a "personal statement." It is important to understand what the point of this final step is. You aren't in high school anymore. This is not the place to focus on your achievements and accolades, which you'll have had the opportunity to note elsewhere on the application.

Rather, your personal statement is where you illustrate that you will be a productive researcher, collaborator, and colleague. Don't lose sight of a fundamental principle about schools, departments, and admissions committees: they are made up of humans. These humans are hoping to find people who will make their life better, while not being overly burdensome. Make it clear that you are just such an appealing applicant.

Take Home Messages

1. While acceptance to professional programs such as medical school, law school, and business school is (usually) impersonal and primarily a function of grades and test scores, acceptance to graduate schools is intensely personal and based on factors beyond just grades and test scores.

2. For PhD programs, you are not just looking for a school. You're also looking for an individual professor who can serve as your official advisor. Because that person will make a significant investment of time and effort into your education and development as a scholar, they play a major role in the decision as to whether you are accepted to the program.

3. Narrow down your options: consider geography and other features of potential schools. Then identify professors doing research that appeals to you. Make positive initial contact and generate a reply. Have a short, substantive exchange on the ideas that motivate you in the field.

4. Do whatever you can to meet with a potential advisor in person. Help them to see that you're a competent, courteous, curious, and interesting student, and that you'll make their life better.

WHAT MAKES YOU AN APPEALING JOB CANDIDATE?

It's Not What You Think

When you're done with college—and probably at some point while you're in college—you'll want to get a job and to thrive in it. Will you know how to do that? Every college has a career center staffed with professionals eager to help students. Going to the career center is a first step that students should take early in their college career.

What does it take to be a great employee? Strong academic training, high IQ, and a good work ethic? Perhaps. But these attributes are neither sufficient nor required. From one of Terry's first employment experiences, we can learn how that can be true.

During high school, Terry worked as a lifeguard at the local public pool. Every week, the head lifeguard, named Destiny, made the work schedule for the upcoming week. The pool was open from 7am until 10pm and the two main shifts were 7am to 3pm and 2pm to 10pm.

Once, when Destiny was taping a new schedule to the guard shack's glass wall, Terry noticed that it could be improved. Lisa, another lifeguard, preferred to work in the morning but had been scheduled for afternoon shifts. Conversely, lifeguard Dave was scheduled for mornings even though he had a second job that often required him to be away from the pool in the morning.

Terry said, "Hey Destiny, if you switch Lisa and Dave, you can make them both happier. You could also improve the schedule by giving Sylvia the day off on Wednesdays, so that she can help coach the swim meets with her uncle, Jaime."

What was Destiny's response? None. Except that she never spoke to Terry again in the two additional summers they worked together. For the rest of her time as head lifeguard, Destiny continued to produce schedules that made the other lifeguards unhappy.

Terry was confused. The schedule that he proposed would have been better or the same for every single lifeguard. Only about twenty years later did Terry figure it out. Destiny's sole goal had been to fulfill her responsibilities while working as little as possible.

As perplexing as this seemed to Terry, Destiny (evidently) did not care one iota whether her coworkers were happy. And that was her prerogative! If lifeguard Dave's second job created conflicts for him, he could quit that job, or he could quit his lifeguarding job. In fact, Destiny cared so little for her coworkers that she probably did not even know Dave's name. Terry had made a rookie mistake that had a negative effect on his own personal situation. He had assumed that there was some objective "best" schedule that should be determined.

In a way, Terry's mistake was the same as Destiny's. She did not think about the schedule from the perspective of the other lifeguards. Terry didn't think about the process of *making* the schedule from Destiny's perspective. That caused his own work experience to be worse than it needed to be.

Jay's friend Greg likes to explain how he learned a similarly useful life lesson from his regular and extreme bouts of "Road Rage." Greg's pet peeve is that people often don't use turn signals when making turns or changing lanes. This drives Greg crazy. "It's totally unsafe! And it's actually illegal!" He even found himself chasing after cars and yelling at the turn-signal-impaired drivers. But one day his passenger and good friend, Brett, made a simple (but also profound) statement:

> *Greg, it's not your job to teach everyone a lesson. Yes, you are right about the lane changing thing. But it's not your job.*

Just because you have a productive thought does not mean that you should say it out loud. Read the situation. And accept that people—coworkers, your boss, lab partners, roommates—get to make decisions about their lives. (Even if you are certain that they are underperforming.)

Imagine that someone called you up and said, "Everything you've ever done in your life is shit." How would you respond? What if the person giving you this unsolicited evaluation was Steve Jobs, then the CEO of Apple? Read on and we will return to this story.

The message from the preceding section is that having a good relationship with your boss is central to career success. Being thoughtful about managing the relationship with your boss is important. In the case of the lifeguard schedule, Terry's suggestion would have helped the organization, but not his boss,

Destiny. If Terry had been smarter in thinking about his boss, he would have had a better outcome.

To the extent that you want to help the boss, what should you do? Your first thought might be to take actions that would feel helpful if *you* were the boss. This is likely to be a mistake, however. To understand why, pick two of the following four words to describe yourself:

Bold   Energetic   Quiet   Bashful

These four words are taken from the "Mini-Markers" personality test. Personality is commonly assessed on five dimensions that can be remembered with the mnemonic OCEAN.

O—openness
C—conscientiousness
E—extraversion
A—agreeableness
N—neuroticism

If you are interested in your own personality type, you can find free tests that will score you on each of these dimensions. Personality tests previously took a long time and included a large number of questions. More recently, academics have developed short—yet still surprisingly accurate—tests.

The four words above are taken from one of these newer, short tests. They provide insight into one aspect of personality, the E dimension—Extraversion. In the list above, bold and energetic are associated with extraverts, while quiet and bashful are most common for introverts.

What is the point about such personality tests? The answer is that people are very different. For example, introverts more than extraverts prefer to discuss important topics one-on-one. Extraverts, on the other hand, prefer a group discussion. Now consider two possible options for interacting with your boss and seeking change in a work process.

Option A: Meet one-on-one with your boss. Ask questions about their feelings, and articulate your request that they make the change you desire. Then wait a week to schedule a follow-up meeting.

Option B: Schedule a big group meeting. Debate and discuss the situation directly, soliciting your coworkers' views and promoting direct discussion of your desired change and the alternatives. Then request that the boss make a decision immediately.

Neither option is necessarily better. An introverted boss is likely to prefer Option A and hate Option B. Conversely, an extraverted boss may reject Option A as inefficient, and perhaps even sneaky because of the lack of transparency with private meetings.

Must you become a psychologist so that you can evaluate and act in accordance with your coworkers' OCEAN scores? No. That's not necessary. You will be more successful, however, simply by recognizing that people are **very** different. Assuming that other people have the same personality type as yours is an unwise approach when determining how best to help your boss (and thereby help yourself).

Returning to our earlier story, Steve Jobs did indeed make a recruitment call to computer engineer Bob Belleville and say "Everything you've ever done in your life is shit." Belleville could have yelled at Jobs or hung up. In fact, Bob Belleville didn't do either. Rather, because he understood that Jobs was extremely direct, prone to hyperbole, and often confrontational, Belleville reasoned that he ought not be overly sensitive or offended. He simply listened. Jobs then proceeded to offer him an extremely cool and desirable job at Apple, which Belleville accepted.

Consider the following description of working conditions:

> [A]nd as for the other men, who worked in tank rooms full of steam, and in some of which there were open vats near the level of the floor, their peculiar trouble was that they fell into the vats; and when they were fished out, there was never enough of them left to be worth exhibiting. Sometimes they would be overlooked for days, till all but the bones of them had gone out to the world as Durham's Pure Leaf Lard!

This description is from Upton Sinclair's *The Jungle*, published in 1906. The meatpacking industry of the time included hard work, low pay, unsanitary conditions, and the risk of having your own body packaged and sold as meat.

Most vocations are far from the meatpacking jungle, but it may not always seem that way. After a career playing professional baseball, Joe Garagiola became an announcer and television host for NBC. After serving as the announcer for the 1988 World Series, he quit his NBC job. Garagiola was interviewed soon afterward, and asked, "Joe, you had the best job in the world. You were paid huge amounts of money to watch baseball, a game you love. Why did you quit?" Joe answered, "You take a man's money, you take his guff. I just decided not to take any more guff."

Every job has some negative aspects, even watching and talking about baseball for millions of dollars. And while some jobs are terrible and downright dangerous—such as meatpacking in the early twentieth century—others are untenable simply because they require you to take more guff than you can tolerate. That's an evaluation that only you can make.

Consider Wichahpi, a young Ivy League law school graduate, an editor of the Law Review at her school, and a former clerk for Supreme Court Justice Ruth Bader Ginsberg (while Ginsberg served on the United States Court of Appeals). Following her clerkship, Wichahpi had her pick of high-paying jobs, and accepted a job at one of the most prestigious law firms in the country.

It turned out, however, that the fancy law firm that Wichahpi joined was nearly always hired by rich, powerful corporations, and never by the "little guy" with whom Wichahpi most commonly sided. One night, Wichahpi found herself in a conference room persuading blue-collar, hourly workers into signing away certain rights.

Wichahpi and her highly paid colleagues protected her law firm's client's interests expertly as they constructed contracts that were legal, but largely unfavorable to the blue-collar workers. This experience was the final straw for Wichahpi, and led her to quit and, eventually, to leave the practice of law entirely.

Wichahpi quit because she did not agree with her firm's actions, even though those actions were legal. We understand that it is rarely feasible to simply quit a job at the moment of an injustice or wrong. Nonetheless, it's necessary to understand that in some situations the best choice for you may be to exit as quickly as possible.

———————

What is "networking?" One dictionary definition is: "interacting with other people to exchange information and develop contacts, especially to further one's career." Picture a networking event in your mind. For us, it is standing at a cocktail party, awkwardly holding an *hors d'oeuvres* plate, wearing a poorly written name tag, and talking to strangers.

Some networking does and should involve slightly uncomfortable interactions with people who are not yet your friends. But other networking involves much more natural relationships. An underappreciated truth is that many career opportunities result primarily from having had a positive previous relationship with someone. This may be the most valuable form of networking, and it evolves naturally. Take the example of Julia.

Julia's work-study job didn't have any additional hours available for her to work. She mentioned this while chatting with her lab partner during a psychology class. Her partner happened to know of work opportunities at an educational research center on campus, so she arranged for Julia to be hired in a "temporary" position. After a few months, the researcher who supervised Julia's work declared that he was impressed with her work and offered her a full-time job for the summer.

Today, almost twenty years later, Julia is a successful educational researcher. She attributes much of her success to that fortuitous job opportunity. It led to a recommendation letter, admission to a PhD program in educational psychology at UCLA, and a long-term research position at UCLA. She now runs her own consulting company and can even trace many of her clients today to that first research supervisor.

The more people you know, the more likely you'll get "lucky" and one of them will be able to open just the right door for you. Treat even a trivial job like a more serious responsibility than seems necessary. Imagine that it's one long interview for the job of your dreams many years from now. Because it might be just that.

Julia's experience of getting a life-changing, career-making break from an acquaintance is consistent with the academic literature. An important finding from employment research is that most job opportunities come from what are called "soft contacts." That is, from people you know a bit, but who are not your close friends.

Why are soft contacts more important than close friends for getting jobs? Scholars hypothesize two reasons. First, you have many more soft contacts than close friends. Second, because you typically have very similar experiences and knowledge as your closest friends, you are more likely to learn something unexpected and novel from a soft contact.

Networking is subject to at least two major misconceptions. The first is that you must interact with strangers to network. In fact, you are networking every time you interact with anyone. In Moliere's play *Le Bourgeois Gentilhomme*, Mr. Jourdain exclaims, "Well, what do you know about that! These forty years now I've been speaking in prose without knowing it!" Similarly, you have been networking all your life, even if you did not realize it.

The second networking misconception is that knowing someone well is the key to having them keep you in mind for job opportunities. This seems reasonable but just isn't true. Think about the person from your high school who was the least responsible. Are you going to recommend that person simply because you have known them for years? No. Of course not.

In an ideal introduction, both the employer and the employee feel lucky to have been introduced. So, the key is a positive perception, not necessarily a long history.

Let's return to the classroom and discuss how our advice about being a good employee relates to your success as a student. So far, we have learned:

1. Being a good employee means helping your bosses achieve their goals.
2. People are extremely variable. Your goals may be very different from your bosses' goals.
3. Some situations must be exited as quickly as possible.
4. You have been (and will be) informally networking all your life.

What is the relevance of these messages for college students? First, put yourself into classes where you can excel. If a particular instructor is not going to help you further your goals, you'll have to adjust: leave or accept the costs of your decision to stay.

For the classes where you stay, strive to understand the world from your instructor's point of view. Take some time to get inside their head; "model their world." Try to achieve your goals by making your instructor's life better.

Take Home Messages

1. A key to success is to understand the perspective of other people. To attain **your** goals, focus on enabling people around you—including those who have power over your life—to attain **their** goals.

2. People have different personality types. In order to help people, invest in learning about them. The best approach is to systematically observe behavior. Trust behavior over words.

3. Some situations and organizations are rotten—or at least a bad fit for you. In such situations, leave as quickly as feasible.

4. You are making impressions, positive and negative, on the people around you at all times. Invisible, nonconscious networking may be the key to your next job and even to your entire life.

5. Your instructor may be centrally important to your post-college career. There are two payoffs to understanding and helping the instructor. First, you will get a better grade. Second, the instructor is more likely to help get you a job or get accepted into graduate school.

CONCLUSION

THE BIG PICTURE, REVISITED

If You Remember Just One Lesson Five Years from Now, It's This . . .

Which of the following describes your mental image of a college instructor most closely?

1. **Instructors are arrogant, insensitive, and mostly disinterested scholars**. Overly focused on grades, eager to deduct points for trivial mistakes, and inflexible, they are not generally enthusiastic about helping students.
2. **Instructors are demanding, but caring and inspirational, mentors**. Role models with a unique ability to understand both the world beyond college and the student perspective, instructors are powerful allies, eager to help students.

Which did you pick? Before we discuss, consider two competing theories of business management.

Theory X (that is its real name)—Employees are lazy and dishonest. The boss's job is to hound employees like dogs, and always have the boot ready to enforce discipline.

Theory Y—Employees genuinely desire to help the organization. People derive pleasure from excellence. The boss's job is to empower the employees.

Business scholars have debated *Theory X* versus *Y* for decades. (*Theory Y* is more popular these days.) One important finding, however, is that both views are self-reinforcing. Bosses who treat employees as dishonest and lazy find that their employees tend not to work hard without close supervision. "See," says the *Theory X* manager, "these lazy louts need the stick or they accomplish nothing." Conversely, bosses who seek to empower their employees are frequently astounded by what the employees are able to accomplish. "See," says the *Theory Y* manager, "these eager whizzes just need me to give them sufficient resources and then get out of their way."

Are instructors disinterested scholars or inspiring mentors? The answer is that an instructor can be either, or both, depending in part on individual student behavior. Two students sitting next to each other in a course, with identical grades, can have wildly different relationships with the same instructor.

As we've seen, the relationships you have and the outcomes you experience depend on you, the choices you make, and the actions you take. This is true to a much greater degree than you ever imagined.

Consider your actions from the instructor's viewpoint. Imagine their view from the podium. Be vigilant for ways to make their lives better. Make a friend or an ally whenever possible, and take care to not make an enemy.

Which of these do you think is a more satisfying conversation for an instructor?

> **Conversation A:** *"If you look at the syllabus, you can see that regrade requests must be submitted within one week of the return of the test. I am sorry, but yours is late. It would be unfair to other*

students to not apply the same rule to you, so your grade of B+ must remain."

Or:

Conversation B: *"Your question about unintended consequences of biotech companies' DNA editing is intriguing. By the way, one of my former students, the CEO of a biotech firm working with this 'CRISPR' technology, is giving a lecture on campus next week. Would you like to join me and a group of graduate students afterward at a lunch with her?"*

Sometimes an action that will literally take you five minutes can set you on a positive course. With a positive start, you can more easily stand out from the class and begin to form a positive professional relationship with your instructor. Conversely, resist self-defeating actions that have little or no reward, yet may create a lasting, negative impression.

Instructors spend many years in training, and often have passed up more financially rewarding careers to be in the classroom with you. They find great satisfaction in nurturing promising students, identifying valuable opportunities for them, and taking steps to help them flourish.

"First class used to be a better meal, now it's a better life." So says Dorothy Boyd in the film *Jerry Maguire*. As we all know, flying can be a real hassle. Boarding a flight can include long waits, crowded gate areas within terminals, and struggling to find an empty overhead compartment for your luggage.

For certain customers, however, the process is much more civilized. All airlines have rewards for their frequent flyers, and those in the most valued groups wait in no lines, are whisked to the front of the security line, and board the plane before the masses.

College students can also have two very different types of experiences when they interact with instructors. The basic, "economy" service includes all the rights of a student: be graded fairly, participate in office hours, have respectful communication with instructors, receive advance warning for assignments, and generally be treated well.

There is, however, a higher level of interaction. As with airline frequent-flyer programs, this "better life" is based on a form of loyalty. Unlike frequent-flyer programs, however, the higher level of interaction possible at colleges can get you to a better destination.

Nearly all instructors will write a letter of recommendation for any student who asks. Nothing, however, requires an instructor to go above and beyond the call of duty on behalf of a student by, for example, making a personal call to the recipient of the recommendation letter in addition to mailing the letter.

Membership in this loyalty status group should never lead to a different grade in a course, but benefits will flow through most other areas. These include research opportunities, mentorship, getting into graduate school, getting a job, earning special scholarships, and many more.

Is it fair for instructors to treat students differently? When it comes to grading: no. But when it comes to other areas: yes. Consider, for example, a firm that contacts an instructor seeking job candidates. For the job, attributes beyond the students' test-taking abilities and class performance will be important to the employer.

Charisma, charm, enthusiasm, and being proactive, for example, are all important attributes for success in a job, but rarely a significant part of the college grading process. Accordingly, when suggesting students for jobs, instructors will nominate the best possible future employee, not necessarily the student with the highest grades.

———————————

Throughout *The Secret Syllabus*, we've explored how to be proactive and wise as you craft your college experience, develop professional relationships, excel in learning and performing, increase your resiliency, and set yourself up for success with whatever comes next. Beyond helping you to achieve success in these endeavors, our goal has been to inspire you to learn and to grow.

An important truth (and added bonus) is this: The strategies that you have learned—and the deep understanding that equips you to develop additional strategies on your own—will need very little modification to help you succeed in the world beyond college.

You have already mastered the secrets of efficient productivity, mutually beneficial professional and personal relationships, and an appreciation for the nuances of balancing current and future goals. You have the knowledge and skills now to thrive in any situation. Class dismissed.

Take Home Messages

1. Think about your interactions with instructors (and everyone else in your life) from their perspective, and adjust your behavior to serve their needs. The better you are able to do this, the better you will be able to succeed.

2. Doing well in college, as in life, involves learning some strategies and techniques. But it also involves deep engagement with the substance. The ability to navigate the alien culture of college well, to form strong relationships, to work hard, and to make wise decisions, will prepare you for the rest of your life.

3. Instructors are people. Model their world. Get inside their head. Truly take their perspective. To the extent that you are able to do this, you will succeed. Academic guidance, mentoring, job opportunities, and more can be bestowed upon you by an instructor who is on your side.

Acknowledgments

We owe a tremendous debt of gratitude to Peter Dougherty, our editor at Princeton University Press. Enthusiastic, wise, and insightful, he shares our passion for helping students flourish in college and beyond. Peter helped us rewrite the book, and guided us to publication masterfully.

Michael Cooperson has provided provocation and wisdom for more than two decades, across all of the topics we cover, with particularly strong guidance for the "How to study a language" chapter, based on his extensive expertise in the field.

Marian Gabra, the Director of University Studies within UCLA's Division of Undergraduate Education, has warmly welcomed Jay to the faculty of the course "Critical Strategies to Achieve Undergraduate Excellence." Thanks also go to Rachel Kennison and Jess Gregg, of UCLA's Center for Education Innovation & Learning in the Sciences, who collaborated with Jay in teaching the course. The book includes numerous ideas and insights garnered from all three of these inspiring educators. Several classes of UCLA students used an earlier draft of the book and provided helpful suggestions.

Many friends, colleagues, and family members have provided valuable input during the gestation and writing of this book, including Elizabeth and Bob Bjork, Sean Dusselier, Erin Enderlin, Neil Garg, Paul Greenberg, Andrew Lo, Ryan Marhoefer, Alicia Moretti, Kevin Phelan, Patrick Phelan, Michelle Richmond, Sheri Snavely, Brian Swartz, Sara Tenney, Bill U'Ren, Anna Zayakina, and Alon Ziv. And from UCLA's Department of Life Sciences Core Education, we thank Tracy Johnson, Deb Pires, Rana Khankan, Frank Laski, and Beth Lazazzera for their support. We also thank Michelle Garceau Hawkins for her excellent copyediting and other suggestions.

Jay would like to thank Charlie, Jack, and Sam for all they have taught me about teaching and learning. And most of all, I thank Julia, for your deep, nuanced expertise in the science of learning and infinite willingness to share it with me, and for your passionate, unwavering devotion to this book.

Terry would like to thank his wife, Barbara, for working together on research and teaching for years. Our daughters, Charlotte, Violet, and Ivy have benefitted from the wisdom contained in this book.

Appendix

RESEARCH CITED AND
SUGGESTED FURTHER READINGS

3. Planning Your Schedule: This Term,
This Year, and through Graduation

- In a study at Harvard, the vast majority of students taking this "eat my vegetables first" approach said that they regretted the decision.

Light, Richard J. *Making the Most of College: Students Speak Their Minds*. Harvard University Press, 2004.

- Surprisingly, such (part-time) jobs do not reduce grades. Moreover, three-quarters of working students say that their work has a positive effect on their overall college satisfaction. They also report that this work does not have a negative impact on their social experiences.

Horn, Laura J., and Jennifer Berktold. *Profile of Undergraduates in US Postsecondary Education Institutions: 1995–96. With an Essay on Undergraduates Who Work. Statistical Analysis Report*. US Government Printing Office, Superintendent of Documents, Mail Stop: SSOP, Washington, DC 20402-9328. 1998.

Lucas, Rosemary, and Norma Lammont. "Combining work and study: an empirical study of full-time students in school, college and university." *Journal of Education and Work* 11.1 (1998): 41–56.

Tessema, Mussie T., Kathryn J. Ready, and Marzie Astani. "Does part-time job affect college students' satisfaction and academic performance (GPA)? The case of a mid-sized public university." *International Journal of Business Administration* 5.2 (2014): 50–59.

Wang, Hongyu, et al. "The effects of doing part-time jobs on college student academic performance and social life in a Chinese society." *Journal of Education and Work* 23.1 (2010): 79–94.

▪ Among the extracurricular activities associated with the highest student happiness are those in the arts. Students report high satisfaction not just for those positions that serve as training for careers or future work in the arts, but also for activities that are fulfilling and pleasurable in their own right.

Astin, Alexander W. "Student involvement: A developmental theory for higher education." *Journal of College Student Personnel* 25.4 (1984): 297–308.

Çivitci, Asım. "Perceived stress and life satisfaction in college students: Belonging and extracurricular participation as moderators." *Procedia-Social and Behavioral Sciences* 205 (2015): 271–281.

Kaur, Dalwinder, and Gurwinder Singh Bhalla. "College management: Views of students." *IUP Journal of Management Research* 9.5 (2010): 6–26.

See also:

Abrahamowicz, Daniel. "College involvement, perceptions, and satisfaction: A study of membership in student organizations." *Journal of College Student Development* 29.3 (1988): 233–238.

Montelongo, Ricardo. "Student participation in college student organizations: A review of literature." *Journal of the Student Personnel Association at Indiana University* (2002): 50–63.

■ Successful college students most often list "effective time management" as central to their success. Students who fail in college rank "poor time management" near the top of their problems.

Britton, Bruce K., and Abraham Tesser. "Effects of time-management practices on college grades." *Journal of Educational Psychology* 83.3 (1991): 405–410.

Claessens, Brigitte J.C., et al. "A review of the time management literature." *Personnel Review* 36.2 (2007): 255–276.

George, Darren, et al. "Time diary and questionnaire assessment of factors associated with academic and personal success among university undergraduates." *Journal of American College Health* 56.6 (2008): 706–715.

Macan, Therese H., et al. "College students' time management: Correlations with academic performance and stress." *Journal of Educational Psychology* 82.4 (1990): 760–768.

■ Finally, do not short-change yourself when it comes to sleep. In a study of the Stanford men's basketball team, researchers evaluated a wide range of measures of athletic performance.

Mah, Cheri D., et al. "The effects of sleep extension on the athletic performance of collegiate basketball players." *Sleep* 34.7 (2011): 943–950.

■ Among the most well-documented and consistent findings across carefully controlled research on sleep are the following.

Gaultney, Jane F. "The prevalence of sleep disorders in college students: Impact on academic performance." *Journal of American College Health* 59.2 (2010): 91–97.

Lund, Hannah G., et al. "Sleep patterns and predictors of disturbed sleep in a large population of college students." *Journal of Adolescent Health* 46.2 (2010): 124–132.

Pilcher, June J., and Amy S. Walters. "How sleep deprivation affects psychological variables related to college students' cognitive performance." *Journal of American College Health* 46.3 (1997): 121–126.

■ Researchers have found that studying in short bursts is associated with inefficiency and poor outcomes.

Allen, George J., Wayne M. Lerner, and James J. Hinrichsen. "Study behaviors and their relationships to test anxiety and academic performance." *Psychological Reports* 30.2 (1972): 407–410.

Michaels, James W., and Terance D. Miethe. "Academic effort and college grades." *Social Forces* 68.1 (1989): 309–319.

See also:

Ericsson, K. Anders, Ralf T. Krampe, and Clemens Tesch-Römer. "The role of deliberate practice in the acquisition of expert performance." *Psychological Review* 100.3 (1993): 363–406.

Gortner Lahmers, Amy, and Carl R. Zulauf. "Factors associated with academic time use and academic performance of college students: A recursive approach." *Journal of College Student Development* 41.5 (2000): 544–556.

Zimmerman, Barry J. "Academic studying and the development of personal skill: A self-regulatory perspective." *Educational Psychologist* 33.2–3 (1998): 73–86.

■ Research has also found that exclusively studying alone is associated with reduced effectiveness.

Hinrichsen, James J. "Prediction of grade point average from estimated study behaviors." *Psychological Reports* 31.3 (1972): 974.

Maloof, Joan, and Vanessa KB White. "Team study training in the college biology laboratory." *Journal of Biological Education* 39.3 (2005): 120–124.

Reynolds, Katherine C., and F. Ted Hebert. "Learning achievements of students in cohort groups." *The Journal of Continuing Higher Education* 46.3 (1998): 34–42.

6. In Choosing Your Courses Seek Great Teachers

■ "More than 50 years ago, leading researchers produced a seminal 746-page report filled with empirical evidence about what works and what doesn't work in education . . . One of the key conclusions of this report is that teacher quality has a big effect on student performance."

Coleman, James Samuel. *Equality of educational opportunity (Coleman) study (EEOS), 1966*. Vol. 6389. Inter-university Consortium for Political and Social Research, 1995.

- In one of the most widely cited papers on this topic, researcher Howard Wachtel summarized: "[A]fter nearly seven decades of research on the use of student evaluations of teaching effectiveness, it can safely be stated that the majority of researchers believe that student ratings are a valid, reliable, and worthwhile means of evaluating teaching."

  Wachtel, Howard K. "Student evaluation of college teaching effectiveness: A brief review." *Assessment & Evaluation in Higher Education* 23.2 (1998): 191–212.

See also:

  Feldman, Kenneth A. "Identifying exemplary teachers and teaching: Evidence from student ratings." *The Scholarship of Teaching and Learning in Higher Education: An Evidence-based Perspective*. Springer, Dordrecht, 2007. 93–143.

  Marsh, Herbert W. "Students' evaluations of university teaching: Research findings, methodological issues, and directions for future research." *International Journal of Educational Research* 11.3 (1987): 253–388.

- Conversely, researchers have found a strong relationship— reported as a correlation of 0.52—between college satisfaction and the number of low-enrollment courses taken.

  Light, Richard J. *Making the Most of College: Students Speak Their Minds*. Harvard University Press, 2004.

See also:

  Cuseo, Joe. "The empirical case against large class size: Adverse effects on the teaching, learning, and retention of first-year students." *The Journal of Faculty Development* 21.1 (2007): 5–21.

- Robust evidence documents that the benefits of high teacher quality extend beyond grades, including improved employment outcomes and higher salaries as well.

  Hanushek, Eric A. "The economic value of higher teacher quality." *Economics of Education Review* 30.3 (2011): 466–479.

  Hanushek, Eric A., and Steven G. Rivkin. "Teacher quality." *Handbook of the Economics of Education* 2 (2006): 1051–1078.

  Rockoff, Jonah E. "The impact of individual teachers on student achievement: Evidence from panel data." *American Economic Review* 94.2 (2004): 247–252.

- In a 2009, Professors Oreopoulos and Hoffmann published "Professor Qualities and Student Achievement." They reported that, "We find that differences in commonly observed instructor traits, such as rank, faculty status, and salary, have virtually no effect on student outcomes. . . . What does matter is instructors' perceived effectiveness and related subjective measures of quality evaluated by students."

  Hoffmann, Florian, and Philip Oreopoulos. "Professor qualities and student achievement." *The Review of Economics and Statistics* 91.1 (2009): 83–92.

- A second study, published in 2010 by Professors Carrell and West, used a similar methodology but with two twists. First, in a design similar to a medical clinical trial, students were randomly assigned to the different instructors. Second, this report examined both the short-term and the long-term impact of professor's attributes.

Carrell, Scott E., and James E. West. "Does professor quality matter? Evidence from random assignment of students to professors." *Journal of Political Economy* 118.3 (2010): 409–432.

10. How to Study (The Lessons You Need but Never Got)

▪ Researchers have quantified just how hard it is to study by measuring "cognitive effort." (This is measured as the degree of interference that performing one task causes in completing a secondary task.)

Piolat, Annie, Thierry Olive, and Ronald T. Kellogg. "Cognitive effort during note taking." *Applied Cognitive Psychology* 19.3 (2005): 291–312.

See also:

Britton, Bruce K., and Abraham Tesser. "Effects of prior knowledge on use of cognitive capacity in three complex cognitive tasks." *Journal of Verbal Learning and Verbal Behavior* 21.4 (1982): 421–436.

Piolat, Annie. "Effects of note-taking and working-memory span on cognitive effort and recall performance." *Writing and Cognition*. Brill, 2007. 109–124.

▪ What makes class notes effective? The answer isn't particularly surprising. It has to do with turning note-taking into an active, rather than passive, process, and making note-taking part of your learning of the material. (Because a great deal of rigorous educational research on this question has produced unambiguous findings, we have high confidence that it is true).

Carter, John F., and Nicholas H. Van Matre. "Note taking versus note having." *Journal of Educational Psychology* 67.6 (1975): 900–904.

Foos, Paul W., Joseph J. Mora, and Sharon Tkacz. "Student study techniques and the generation effect." *Journal of Educational Psychology* 86.4 (1994): 567–576.

Isaacs, Geoff. "Lecturing practices and note-taking purposes." *Studies in Higher Education* 19.2 (1994): 203–216.

Titsworth, B. Scott. "The effects of teacher immediacy, use of organizational lecture cues, and students' notetaking on cognitive learning." *Communication Education* 50.4 (2001): 283–297.

Williams, Robert L., and Alan C. Eggert. "Notetaking in college classes: Student patterns and instructional strategies." *The Journal of General Education* 51.3 (2002): 173–199.

■ Hundreds of research studies have evaluated the value of using practice tests versus restudy. Their overwhelming finding is that practice testing results in a significant improvement on final exam performance, typically thirty percent or more.

Karpicke, Jeffrey D., and Janell R. Blunt. "Retrieval practice produces more learning than elaborative studying with concept mapping." *Science* 331.6018 (2011): 772–775.

Karpicke, Jeffrey D., and Henry L. Roediger. "The critical importance of retrieval for learning." *Science* 319.5865 (2008): 966–968.

Roediger III, Henry L., and Jeffrey D. Karpicke. "Test-enhanced learning: Taking memory tests improves long-term retention." *Psychological Science* 17.3 (2006): 249–255.

- Evidence from rigorous research studies revealed that students using the "elaborative interrogation" method of studying performed about forty percent better on their final exam than students who only read and reread their notes.

  Dunlosky, John, et al. "Improving students' learning with effective learning techniques: Promising directions from cognitive and educational psychology." *Psychological Science in the Public Interest* 14.1 (2013): 4–58.

See also:

  deWinstanley, Patricia Ann, and Robert A. Bjork. "Successful lecturing: Presenting information in ways that engage effective processing." *New Directions for Teaching and Learning* 2002.89 (2002): 19–31.

  Seifert, Timothy L. "Effects of elaborative interrogation with prose passages." *Journal of Educational Psychology* 85.4 (1993): 642–651.

- In one well-controlled study, researchers found that students' accuracy on practice problems was close to thirty percent higher when blocking. When course exams include material from multiple topics, however, it turns out that students using interleaved practice score significantly better. In the same study, the exam scores of students using interleaving during their studying were forty percent higher than those using blocked practice.

  Rohrer, Doug, and Kelli Taylor. "The shuffling of mathematics problems improves learning." *Instructional Science* 35.6 (2007): 481–498.

See also:

Taylor, Kelli, and Doug Rohrer. "The effects of interleaved practice." *Applied Cognitive Psychology* 24.6 (2010): 837–848.

■ For different exams, students used either blocked or interleaved practice. When they were asked to judge their exam performance, more than sixty percent believed they performed better using blocked practice, while only twenty percent believed they performed better with interleaving. (The remaining students believed there was no difference.)

Kornell, Nate, and Robert A. Bjork. "Learning concepts and categories: Is spacing the 'enemy of induction'?" *Psychological Science* 19.6 (2008): 585–592.

■ This is called "the spacing effect" and it turns out to be one of the most consistent and well-documented phenomena in all of educational research.

Bahrick, Harry P., and Lynda K. Hall. "The importance of retrieval failures to long-term retention: A metacognitive explanation of the spacing effect." *Journal of Memory and Language* 52.4 (2005): 566–577.

Hintzman, Douglas L. "Theoretical implications of the spacing effect." In *Theories in Cognitive Psychology: The Loyola Symposium*, edited by R. L. Solso, 77–99. Lawrence Erlbaum (1974).

Kornell, Nate. "Optimising learning using flashcards: Spacing is more effective than cramming." *Applied Cognitive Psychology: The Official Journal of the Society for Applied Research in Memory and Cognition* 23.9 (2009): 1297–1317.

Pavlik Jr, Philip I., and John R. Anderson. "Practice and forgetting effects on vocabulary memory: An activation-based model of the spacing effect." *Cognitive Science* 29.4 (2005): 559–586.

Sisti, Helene M., Arnold L. Glass, and Tracey J. Shors. "Neurogenesis and the spacing effect: Learning over time enhances memory and the survival of new neurons." *Learning & Memory* 14.5 (2007): 368–375.

Smith, Christopher D., and Damian Scarf. "Spacing repetitions over long timescales: A review and a reconsolidation explanation." *Frontiers in Psychology* 8 (2017): 962.

12. Papers and Other Writing Assignments: Say It Better

Pinker, Steven. *The Sense of Style: The Thinking Person's Guide to Writing in the 21ˢᵗ Century*. Penguin Books, 2015.

White, Elwyn Brooks, and William Strunk. *The Elements of Style*. Macmillan, 1972.

14. Resilience: Everyone Falls; Only Some Get Back Up

■ In the *Journal of Behavioral Decision Making*, researchers described experimental results with serious practical value. People who contemplated their emotions—particularly their bad feelings associated with a failure—were better able to correct their mistakes in subsequent efforts.

Nelson, Noelle, Selin A. Malkoc, and Baba Shiv. "Emotions know best: The advantage of emotional versus cognitive responses to failure." *Journal of Behavioral Decision Making* 31.1 (2018): 40–51.

- One scientific study asked people who were HIV-positive to write about their feelings. Patients who were more expressive in exploring their emotional response to their condition were healthier.

Rivkin, Inna D., et al. "The effects of expressive writing on adjustment to HIV." *AIDS and Behavior* 10.1 (2006): 13–26.

17. What Makes You an Appealing Job Candidate? It's Not What You Think

- According to employment research, most job opportunities come from what are called "soft contacts."

English, Fenwick W. *The Postmodern Challenge to the Theory and Practice of Educational Administration*. Charles C. Thomas Publisher, 2003.

Granovetter, Mark S. "The strength of weak ties." *American Journal of Sociology* 78.6 (1973): 1360–1380.

Index